ANDY JONES & ARTHUR DICK

1001 GUITAR
Tips & Tricks

WISE PUBLICATIONS
London/New York/Paris/Sydney/Madrid/Copenhagen

Exclusive Distributors:
MUSIC SALES LIMITED
8/9 Frith Street,
London W1V 5TZ, England.
MUSIC SALES PTY LIMITED
120 Rothschild Avenue,
Rosebery, NSW 2018,
Australia.
MUSIC SALES CORPORATION
257 Park Avenue South,
New York,
NY10010,
United States of America.

Order No. AM91532
ISBN 0-7119-3754-0
This book © Copyright 1995 by Wise Publications

Compiled and edited by Andy Jones and Arthur Dick
Music processed by Seton Music Graphics

Cover design by Pearce Marchbank, Studio Twenty
Text photographs courtesy of London Features International

Printed in the United Kingdom by
Caligraving Limited, Thetford, Norfolk.

YOUR GUARANTEE OF QUALITY
As publishers, we strive to produce every book to the
highest commercial standards.
The music has been freshly engraved and throughout, the
printing and binding have been planned to ensure a sturdy,
attractive publication which should give years of enjoyment.
Particular care has been given to specifying acid-free,
neutral-sized paper made from pulps which have not been
elemental chlorine bleached. This pulp is from farmed
sustainable forests and was produced with special
regard for the environment.
If your copy fails to meet our high standards,
please inform us and we will gladly replace it.

Music Sales' complete catalogue describes thousands of titles
and is available in full colour sections by subject, direct from
Music Sales Limited. Please state your areas of interest and
send a cheque/postal order for £1.50 for postage to:
Music Sales Limited, Newmarket Road,
Bury St. Edmunds, Suffolk IP33 3YB.

INTRODUCTION

This book is not a method book nor is it aimed at one specific type of player or one specific standard of accomplishment. It is a compendium of ideas, some more weighty than others.

The best way to use *1001 Guitar Tips & Tricks* is to dip into it when the mood takes you. You should be able to open it at any point and find something of interest.

Nowadays we have reached a point where different musical styles are converging, due partly to the availability of modern recordings. Many of the main styles of music are undergoing subtle changes – influenced by seemingly very different musical forms.

If your particular style is not given a large amount of space it is due to the fact that I've tried to provide a range of ideas across the more popular areas of guitar playing.

I must at this point make my apologies to left handed players. Throughout the text the player is addressed as a right-hander. If you are left handed you'll realise that when I talk of left hand technique, I'm talking about the fretting hand (as opposed to the plucking hand). So what I've called left hand exercises are for you right hand exercises.

The technical exercises contained within should be quite sufficient for any level of technique and even beginners could take on one page of both left hand and right hand exercises every week.

Throughout the notation based section I've used tablature. My own feeling is that if you're energetic enough to want to decipher TAB, you might as well get to grips with conventional music notation. This conventional notation is universal so you can read music originally intended for a wide range of different instruments.

On the other hand, a great benefit of TAB is that it provides a clear indication of where notes are to be played.

Music from the repertoire of other instruments can be a great eye opener for guitar players. One of my favourite piano players is Bill Evans. His playing sounds so full that you'd think his approach has no relevance to guitarists. However, with a little consideration and a few omissions you can apply much of his chordal thinking to the guitar. There's so much great music out there – why limit yourself?

ANDY JONES

GUITAR BASICS
BUYING AN INSTRUMENT

Many of the basic 'rules' of buying an instrument pertain to both ends of the market although some are aimed exclusively at the inexperienced player:

1 It's best to buy from a dealer who has a good reputation in your area.

2 You must be careful that you're buying an instrument that is meant to cater for the style of music you're playing. If you're really obsessed with heavy metal guitar playing, I can't imagine you're going to get the sounds you crave from a classical guitar.

3 Shop around if you can and don't be in too much of a hurry. 'Buy in haste, repent at your leisure'!!!

4 Communication is important. You must take the time to explain to the salesman EXACTLY what you require the instrument to do.

5 Watch out for any instrument with rough fret edges.

6 Buy an instrument with a weather proof case – some instruments are held together with water soluble glue!

7 If you use a gig bag or soft case, try to get one which has some form of padding. Just a little bit will make all the difference.

8 Use a comfortable strap, especially if your guitar is (physically) heavy.

9 Don't be bullied into buying something – the salesman may know just as little as you do.

10 As a general guideline, an expensive new item by a major name manufacturer will hold its value much better than a similar priced product from a little known company. You may unexpectedly find a need to sell it for one reason or another, who knows.

11 It generally pays to buy the best instrument you can afford.

  1. You'll enjoy playing more because it will sound so good,

  2. you'll have no excuses.

12 On the other hand there's no point in spending thousands on a piece of gear if it means you have to get a job working behind a bar to pay for it.

13 Be aware of the strengths/weaknesses of any equipment you are thinking of buying.

14 Find out what are considered to be the best combinations of gear. For instance, my Fender Telecaster sounds amazing through a Fender Twin Reverb but I can't get the type of jazz sound I want from the same amp with an Ibanez Artist guitar.

15 You may have to tailor the kind of amp you use not only to the type of sound you want but also to the type of venues you play. A Marshall stack sounds great at high volume but it's no good to you in a jazz wine bar duo.

16 If you're tempted to buy a powerful valve amp because one of the gods of Rock 'n' Roll says he uses it –

BE CAREFUL. Most valve amps need to be turned up pretty loud before they start giving a really beefy distortion. This level may very well be too loud for the kind of gigs you're doing.

17 If the last tip rang some alarm bells, consider using a distortion pedal or effects unit with built-in distortion.

18 If you live in a house where practising is not possible, or if your only practise time comes when respectable people are asleep, you could try using a headphone amp.

19 With headphone amps and beginner level practise amps I would suggest that, if you can afford to, you should buy one with reverb, delay or even chorus. The sound of a cheap amp with nothing to smooth out the tone can be pretty unforgiving.

20 If you're buying second-hand equipment it's sometimes worth being just a little cynical. Check the music press or local papers to try to work out what the going rate is. Second-hand equipment is obviously going to be more expensive from a music shop but their guarantee might be worth a premium.

21 If you buy second-hand gear from a shop you should find out what kind of guarantee they're offering – how long it lasts and the type of cover.

22 If you're buying a second-hand valve amplifier, be aware that valves have a limited life span – after a certain amount of use the tone will deteriorate. Therefore, the amp that sounds like a bargain could end up costing you more if you find the valves are shot. You'll have to use your ears when you test any valve amp.

23 When buying a classical guitar look down the length of the neck to make sure there is no irregular or extreme curvature.

24 Make sure that if there are very bright stage lights you do not leave your instrument in their beam for long periods. On one gig I did recently the lights were so bright the finish on the back of the neck of my guitar started to melt.

TUNING

25 The guitar can be tuned with the aid of pitch pipes or dedicated electronic guitar tuners which are available through your local music dealer.

If you do not have a tuning device, you can use relative tuning.

Press down where indicated, one at a time, following the instructions.

Estimate the pitch of the 6th string as near as possible to E or at least a comfortable pitch (not too high, as you might break other strings in tuning up).

Then, while checking the various positions on the diagram, place a finger from your left hand on the:

5th fret of the E or 6th string and **tune the open A** (or 5th string) to the note A.

5th fret of the A or 5th string and **tune the open D** (or 4th string) to the note D.

5th fret of the D or 4th string and **tune the open G** (or 3rd string) to the note G.

4th fret of the G or 3rd string and **tune the open B** (or 2nd string) to the note B.

5th fret of the B or 2nd string and **tune the open E** (or 1st string) to the note E.

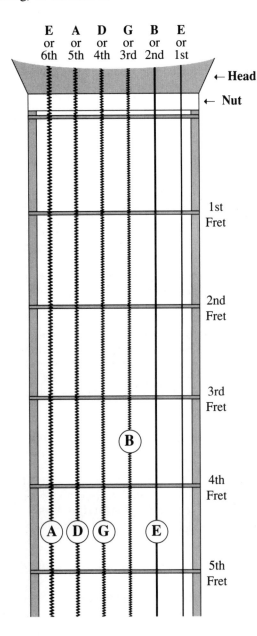

YOUR INSTRUMENT AND ACCESSORIES

26 Set your pickups fairly close to the strings but check the high notes will sustain. If the strings are too close to the pickups the magnetic pull will choke the vibration of the strings.

27 If you have to replace any fuses in your gear, always keep some spares to hand. If the fuse blew once, chances are it will happen again.

28 Always carry spare strings – the rest of the band will never forgive you if a string breaks and you can't continue the gig.

29 Certain guitars with Floyd Rose style whammy bars need strings with the ball end chopped off. Chop them off before going to the gig, it saves messing about with a pair of pliers.

30 When re-stringing your guitar, wind the string through the hole and turn the peg so that the string passes over the hole.

When the string winds through again make sure it passes under the level of the hole. This puts pressure on the string to stay in place.

31 Use a string cleaner – it will save you buying new strings by cleaning any accumulated grease and dirt before it turns to rust.

32 If the guitar's jack socket comes loose, don't just tighten it up – you'll pull the wires out inside. Instead, hold the socket in place by putting a thin nosed pair of pliers into it, while tightening the nut with your other hand.

33 If the jack socket points out from your guitar at 90 degrees, use an angled head jack cable, especially if the guitar is a semi-acoustic one. The danger of tugging the socket is too great to risk.

34 Tuck your cable over the strap so that the weight of the guitar holds it in place. This means you won't pull the cable out if you step on it.

35 Use a strap lock, especially if you've splashed out on an expensive shiny guitar.

36 Raise your speakers up off the floor – you'll damp a lot of their projection by putting them on the ground. Also, by raising them higher to your head you'll be able to hear yourself more easily without having to turn the level up.

37 Keep a spare plectrum in your guitar case and your jacket, trousers *etc*. It's very embarrassing when you get to a gig and set up only to find you've forgotten your pick.

38 Never leave your guitar near any kind of heat source – others might not be aware of the danger inherent in turning the fire on!

39 If it's at all possible, refrain from leaving your guitar in a very dry or very hot room. When the moisture leaves the wood it will contract. This will result in bowing of the neck. Acoustic guitars are particularly prone to cracking due to extreme humidity/temperature changes.

40 If you live in a hot dry climate you can try to offset these adverse effects by leaving a large bowl of water close to the guitar.

41 If you're travelling, it's possible to buy a humidifier which can be left inside your case or even inside your guitar.

42 Every now and again check the mains connections to your equipment to ensure the wiring and fuses are secure.

AT REHEARSALS/GIGS

43 Mark your name and address/phone number on all your gear, especially cables and accessories. So many of these items are standard issue that confusion can easily arise as to their ownership. This kind of situation often comes about at gigs where you have to vacate the stage quickly to make way for another band.

44 If you're stacking equipment in a car or van, pack speaker cabinets face down on a flat surface – this will prevent any damage to the grille or speakers.

45 Insure your gear.

46 Never leave any of your gear in any vehicle – the chances of it getting stolen are too great to risk. Also you might find even if the insurance company pays up, you can't really replace that old guitar you've had for years.

47 If you find there's no sound coming out of your amp set-up, try out all your cables. Eliminate each one by plugging it straight into the amp, not through the effects.

48 Don't leave drinks on top of your amplifier – it's an accident waiting to happen.

49 If liquid is spilled on any of your electrical equipment, take your guitar off without touching any metal parts and switch off AT THE MAINS.

50 Don't leave your guitar leaning against a chair. If you're not using it either put it on a guitar stand or back in the case.

51 Most guitars these days (except classical guitars) come equipped with a truss rod. This is a strong metal bar running through the neck of the instrument. It is slightly curved and when turned it adjusts the curvature of the neck. You'll need an Allen key to adjust this. The truss rod is generally found under a badge near the nut. If your strings are buzzing in one particular place on the neck of the instrument, you may find a truss rod adjustment will sort it out. Adjust the truss rod in increments of 1/4 of a turn.

52 If there's a local music shop with a reputable repairman, it's definitely worth getting your guitar 'set up'. This means the height of the strings and the curvature of the neck. The height of the pickups will be (hopefully) adjusted to suit your style of playing.

53 If you use a whammy bar make sure it's accessible when you need it. There's normally some sort of mechanism for securing it.

TRAVELLING

54 Use a safety belt to secure your guitar flightcase. Clasps are often knocked open in transit.

55 If your instrument gets damaged in transit, be sure to register your claim with the airline before you leave the airport.

56 Get written confirmation that the accident has been registered.

57 Don't leave your guitar in a gig bag in the back of a van. It WILL fall over and it WILL get damaged.

EFFECTS UNITS

58 When using effects units, pedals or rack mounted, you'll find the best way to use them is to plug them into your amplifier's send and return sockets. Certain units like the Alesis Quadraverb (great unit that it is!) have a very low output signal if you plug directly through it.

59 Always use the best cables you can afford.

60 Use designated guitar cables for guitar to amp/fx and speaker cables for speakers.

61 You'll find it's worth getting short cables to connect the units in your rack. If you use standard length cables you're likely to get everything into a horrible tangle.

62 Read the manual when you get a new effects box – you'll only get the best out of a unit when you understand how it works.

63 One very important function on modern multi-effects units is the effects mix. By altering the amount of output which comes from each effect you have a lot of control   over the 'shape' of your sound.

64 When it comes to buying an effects unit, it's worth thinking about the way you approach learning about such devices. If you're the sort of person who likes to just plug in, dial up a sound and play, then certain of the more modern devices may demand more effort than you're prepared to put in. A simpler device might be sufficient for your needs.

65 When you're setting up your effects units make sure the actual volume is fairly balanced between clean and distorted sounds. This may entail lowering the volume on your distortion unit.

66 If you use a foot switch or midi foot controller to send program changes to your amp and effects, be sure that you can remember which button calls up which sounds. It can really throw you when an unexpected tone comes out.

67 Try using a volume pedal to fade chords in and out – it adds atmosphere to your accompaniments.

68 If you do use a volume pedal you might try putting it between your pre-amp (if you use one) and power amp. This way you won't lose any of the quality or gain of the pre-amp's tone. This is especially relevant to distorted sounds.

69 If you normally use a lot of delay or reverb it's probably worth creating an effects setting which has just a dry signal in case the band comes to a dead stop. It sounds pretty silly when they've stopped and your note is still ringing.

SAFETY PRECAUTIONS

70 When you're putting a new plug on a piece of gear always tighten the screws which hold the cable at the entrance to the plug. Someone could easily step on the plug and put pressure on the wires.

71 Buy a circuit breaker to put between you and your electrical equipment. If you get a shock the power will cut out immediately.

72 Don't fool around with any of your electrical gear while it's plugged in.

73 If you're fitting a plug to a piece of electrical equipment, make sure you strip the individual wires just enough to make a connection. You don't want to risk two wires touching if a cable gets tugged.

READING THE DOTS

74 Musical notes are written on a system of five equally-spaced horizontal lines called a stave. Their position on the stave denotes their pitch.

75 The *higher pitched* notes (normally played by the right hand on a keyboard instrument) are written in the **Treble Clef**, the sign for which appears at the beginning of the stave like this:

76 The Bass Clef is used for the lower pitched (left hand) notes and looks like this:

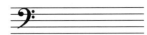

77 Notes are given letter names corresponding to the first seven letters of the alphabet, A to G. This sequence keeps repeating throughout the whole pitch range.

A B C D E F G, A B C D E F G, A B C *etc.*

78 A note is written either *on a line* or *in the space* between two **lines** of the stave. The notes on the **lines** of the treble clef are:

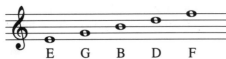
E G B D F

79 and the notes in the **spaces** are:

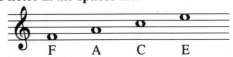
F A C E

80 The notes on the **lines** of the bass clef are:

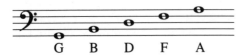
G B D F A

81 and the notes in the **spaces** are:

A C E G

82 Notes which are too high or too low to be placed on the stave are written on short added lines called **Ledger Lines**, which effectively extend the stave upwards or downwards at that point.

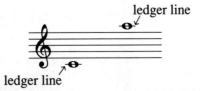
ledger line
ledger line

83 Tip 84 shows the most commonly used notes, with their letter names, written in the treble and bass clefs. The note C which is written on a ledger line either just below the treble clef or just above the bass clef is called **Middle C**, and is found in the middle of the piano keyboard.

84

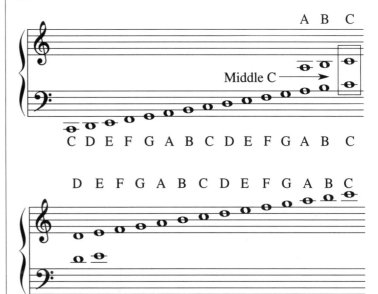

A B C
Middle C
C D E F G A B C D E F G A B C

D E F G A B C D E F G A B C

D E

85 Each note in a piece of music has a specific length or duration in relation to the other notes. The relative duration is indicated by the appearance of the note. Each type of note also has a corresponding symbol called a **Rest**, which indicates a period of silence of equal duration. Here are some of the most common notes and their rests, starting with the longest.

86 A **Semibreve** (Whole Note) lasts twice as long as:

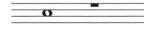

87 A **Minim** (Half Note) which lasts twice as long as:

88 A **Crotchet** (Quarter Note) which lasts twice as long as:

89 A **Quaver** (Eighth Note) which lasts twice as long as:

90 A **Semiquaver** (Sixteenth Note) and so on.

91 Pairs of quavers are often joined by a horizontal line called a **Beam**, and similarly groups of four semiquavers may be joined by a double beam:

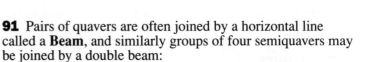

92 Most music has a regular pulse or **Beat**. It is divided by **Bar Lines** into short sections of equal duration called **Bars** (or *Measures*), and each bar in a piece usually contains the same number of beats. Two numbers placed one above the other just after the clef sign at the beginning of the piece comprise the **Time Signature**. The *upper number* gives the *number of beats* in a bar and the *lower* number shows the *value for one beat*.

93 In the following example there are three beats in the bar, and each beat is a *crotchet*. (The number 4 indicates crotchets or quarter notes; if the number were 8 then each beat would be a quaver or eighth note.)

Three beats in a bar
Bar line
Crotchet beat
One bar

94 When a dot is placed after a note it increases its length by half as much again.

95 In the above example the curved line joining the two notes of the *same* pitch is called a **Tie**, and means that the first note is held on for the length of both notes added together without the second one being played. But a curved line joining two or more notes of *different* pitch is called a **Slur**, and means that the notes are to be played smoothly, without any gaps between them.

96 A **Double Bar Line** (often called simply a *double bar*) is used to show the end of a section in a piece of music:

97 At the end of a piece the second bar line is thicker for greater emphasis:

98 If a section of music is to be played twice, it need only be written out once and **Repeat Signs** placed at the beginning and end of it:

99 Sometimes a repeated section has a different ending. In this case **1st and 2nd Time Bars** are used to accommodate the differences.

SCALES AND KEYS

100 The pitch distance between a note and the next nearest note is called a **Semitone**. The distance between a note and the next note but one is a **Tone** (two semitones). There are two main types of scale in Western music, **Major** and **Minor**. The scale of C major is shown here. All the notes in the scale are a tone apart, except for E – F and B – C (marked with slurs), which are a semitone apart.

101 When scales start on notes other than C the same sequence of tones and semitones still has to be maintained. To do this some notes have to be altered (raised or lowered) by using sharps or flats. The following signs can be placed in front of the note.

102 A sharp ♯ raises the note a semitone.

103 A flat ♭ lowers the note a semitone.

104 A natural sign ♮ cancels the effect of a previous sharp or flat.

105 A double-sharp ✕ raises a note a tone (2 semitones).

106 A double flat ♭♭ lowers a note a tone (2 semitones).

107 **Key Signatures** are used at the beginning of each stave to show which key a piece is in, and also to permanently raise or lower the pitch of certain notes to maintain the correct sequence of tones and semitones in the scale. Minor scales use a different sequence of tones and semitones from major. Here is a scale of A minor (melodic form). The sequence of tones and semitones varies depending on whether the scale is ascending or descending.

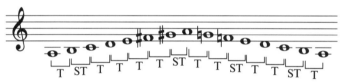

108 The key signatures of all the major and minor keys are shown below:

C major or A minor
(no sharps or flats)

Sharp Keys

G major or E minor

D major or B minor

A major or F♯ minor

E major or C♯ minor

B major or G♯ minor

F♯ major or D♯ minor

C♯ major or A♯ minor

Flat Keys

F major or D minor

B♭ major or G minor

E♭ major or C minor

A♭ major or F minor

D♭ major or B♭ minor

G♭ major or E♭ minor

C♭ major or A♭ minor

109 Compound time is where the basic pulse of the music is subdivided into uneven groups of beats. For instance,   in 6/8 the bars are divided into two groups of three quavers.

110 The 12/8 time signature is much used in guitar music, especially the blues. Here the bars are subdivided into four groups of three quavers each.

111 At moderate tempos in blues music, 12/8 has many similarities with 4/4. It's just that the beats have more of a bouncy feel in 12/8.

112 Musical notation can convey more than just the notes – observe indications as to dynamics, phrasing and form.

113 Guitar chords are displayed as diagrams that represent the fingerboard of the guitar. There are six vertical lines representing the six strings of the guitar. Horizontal lines represent the frets. The strings are arranged with the high E (first, or thinnest) string to the right, and the low E (sixth, or thickest) to the left. The black circles indicate at which fret the finger is to be placed and the number tells you which finger to use. At the top of the diagram there is a thick black line indicating the neck of the guitar. Diagrams for chords up the neck just have a fret line at the top with a Roman numeral to the right to identify the first fret of the diagram. You will occasionally see X's and 0's. An X indicates that the string below it is either not played or damped, an 0 simply means the string is played as an open string.

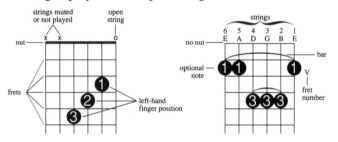

114 If you intend to learn to read music you should acquaint yourself with the meaning of various musical terms (generally French, Italian or German). A basic book of musical theory will furnish you with most of the terms you'll need.

115 If your part in a piece of music contains the indication 'play fills' this means you should add little phrases to support the melody. Try not to get in the way of the main instrument/voice.

116 If a piece of music contains the indication 'double time' (or 'double X'), this means that at this point the pulse of the music doubles in speed.

117 If a piece has the indication 'double time feel' this merely means that the chords and melody go by as written but the underlying groove is double the previous speed.

118 If a piece is a 'swing' tune this means there's a lilt to the quavers. In fact, where you see:–

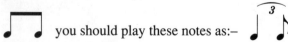 you should play these notes as:–

119 Note that at different tempos, the amount of 'swing' will alter. At very fast tempos the quavers will be forced to sound even – the shorter notes will be too fast to articulate.

120 When you're playing a jazz tune try not to make the quavers sound like

121 If you see this symbol:- ✗ you are instructed to repeat the previous bar. This device saves copyists and composers a good deal of time. It also means your brain isn't analysing the same bar over and over again.

122 When you buy a new book of guitar music it's always important to check out the tab key (the explanation of the different musical symbols for such guitar techniques as bending).

123 The term 'comping' means accompaniment. It's most frequently used in jazz contexts.

124 The symbol for a downstroke of the pick is: ⊓

125 The symbol for an upstroke of the pick is: ∨

126 The symbol for a major 7th chord is: maj7

127 The symbol for a minor 7th chord is: m7

128 The symbol for a diminished chord is: ° or dim

129 The symbol for an augmented chord is: + or aug

130 If you see the + (augmented) sign after a dominant 7th this means the chord has a raised fifth. C7+ (aug) is C7 with the 5th note G, augmented or sharpened to G♯.

131 In classical guitar notation very clear indications as to fingerings are given without the need for tablature. If there is a number within a circle above a note that gives you the number of the string this note should be played on.

132 If there's a number not enclosed in a circle this tells you which left hand finger to use. 1 = index finger.

133 Classical guitar notation gives names to the right hand fingers. The thumb is notated by the symbol 'p', the index finger by 'i', the second finger by 'm', the ring finger by 'a' and the rarely used little finger by 'e'.

SIGHT READING ON THE GUITAR

134 When you first start to read music at sight, progress will be very slow. Patience will definitely bring great rewards. Don't be too ambitious in the material you start off with.

135 Start with books of music intended for beginners. Maybe a book of easy pieces for guitar or even one of the other instruments.

136 If you're interested in getting your sight reading together, one of the best sources of practise material is the repertoire of the clarinet, particularly books of studies or technical exercises.

137 Don't neglect your chord rhythm reading – it's as important as your single line solos.

138 It's crucial that you practise sight reading in time. If you don't you're not doing justice to your sense of time. Save up for a metronome.

139 When you're sight reading try to look ahead of the notes you're just about to play.

MOVEMENT AND IMPROVEMENT

POSTURE

140 This is an example of good classical posture.

John Williams

141 This is how one great rocker holds his guitar – you know this one works !

Eddie Van Halen

142 This is how the very finest country player holds his guitar.

Albert Lee

143 Note how relaxed this great bluesman is when he plays.

Buddy Guy

144 It is very important to realise the need for good posture when you play. Over time, bad posture will inhibit your progress and could eventually lead to fairly serious physical problems.

145 Whichever style of music you're playing try not to allow yourself to slouch or bend your body too far around the instrument.

146 Classical guitar players favour the use of a footrest to support the left leg, thereby raising the instrument higher up the torso and facilitating better access to the instrument. If you're a fingerstyle player (non-classical), it might be worth checking out if a footrest might help your posture.

147 When using a footrest it is advisable to take regular breaks otherwise your leg will 'go to sleep'.

148 If you don't like the idea of using a footrest, it might be worth checking out some of the newer guitar supports which are placed upon the knee to raise the guitar up. (This has found favour with some classical players.)

149 Fingerstyle players should aim to rest the right arm on the guitar. The weight of the arm should be taken by the guitar, there's no need for you to try to hold the arm up. When you feel tension in the arm stop playing for a moment and just relax the arm by your side.

150 If you need to use more than one guitar during the same song, there are guitar stands on the market which hold the instrument at the right height. You merely stand behind the guitar and play. While playing this second guitar, you push the other guitar (suspended on a guitar strap) behind to your back.

151 If you do gigs standing up, make sure that you spend at least some of your practise time standing up. You use the muscles in your arms, back and shoulders in a different way when sitting.

152 If you experience pain in your back and shoulders, you should try stretching exercises to compensate for bunching up your muscles. Tall players must be especially careful when it comes to posture.

153 If you're reading music, position the stand to the left – that's the side of your fretting arm. It's more likely you'll need to keep looking at that hand to check finger placement.

154 Be careful with the length of your strap – if it's hanging down by your knees it might look cool but you're not going to have the best access to the notes. It's a question of fashion versus command of the instrument.

155 Keep as fit as you can – fitness helps keep your attitude positive and maintains the physical mechanism you need to play your instrument.

156 If you want to strengthen your hands practise squeezing fairly hard on a tennis ball or a squash ball if you've got small hands.

157 I would advise you to avoid using any kind of mechanical device which claims to help your playing by straining to squeeze with each finger. Remember, we're actually training our fingers to do their stuff with only the minimum of strain – go back to the tennis ball, it's pretty harmless.

158 If your guitar has a whammy bar the action of bending one string lowers the pitch of the others. Therefore it's basically impossible to bend one note in a chord and keep the others in tune.

TECHNIQUE – LEFT HAND

159 Develop your left hand so that you're only using the weight of the finger to fret the note – any more pressure is merely a waste of effort and inhibits flexibility.

160 The left hand thumb is strongest when placed in the middle of the neck of the guitar, just opposite the second left hand finger.

161 Try to use the tips of your fingers, not the pads, to fret notes. This makes for greater accuracy and reduces the chances of accidentally fretting on more than one string.

162 Avoid an excessive arch in the shape of your wrist. Think how your wrist looks when you pick up something heavy – it's strongest when it's almost straight.

163 Don't let your fingers collapse when you're playing – if they do, you're probably pressing too hard.

164 When you find there's a lot of tension in either your wrist or fingers, you'll very often find that accuracy in the placement of your fingers is the problem, rather than not pressing hard enough to make the notes sound.

165 If you have problems with barré chords, try adjusting the position of your index finger across the strings by moving it slightly towards or away from you. Problems often occur due to the shape of an individual's index finger and it is important that firm contact is made with the string/fret to produce a clean sound.

166 If you suffer from tension in your fingers, then you're obviously overpressing. Spend some time each day experimenting with the minimum amount of finger pressure. The aim is to educate your fingers to accept the fact that their weight alone is sufficient to make any note/chord sound.

167 If you feel discomfort in your arms or fingers, stop playing. I can tell you from bitter experience that practising too hard with bad technique is a big waste of time and can set your playing back months.

168 If you're working on a technical exercise which uses one note, you may end up squeezing too hard. To prevent muscle strain, occasionally change the note.

169 If you're working on the right hand, don't make the left hand perform a complicated set of movements.

170 Even if you're not particularly feeling tension in your hands and arms it's a good idea to get up out of your seat every 20 minutes. Move around and stretch your arms.

171 Try to restrict the amount of movement in your fingers – get them into place ready to play the next note as soon as possible.

172 Barré chord – where the left hand index finger is flattened on the fingerboard to hold down more than one note. E.g.:

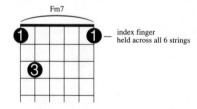

173 Make sure the flesh of the left hand palm or index finger does not make contact (unless you're fretting a barré chord) with the top string. If it does, the top note of your chords will not sound.

174 Be careful with your timing when using pull-offs and hammer-ons. There is a tendency for these devices to be rhythmically sloppy.

175 Practise bending in tune. Try this exercise.

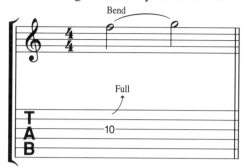

176 Now this:

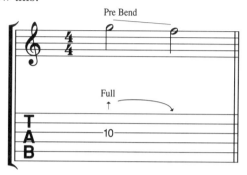

177 Now this:

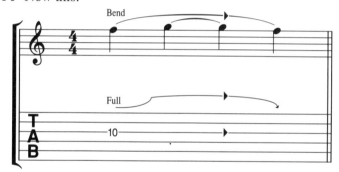

RIGHT HAND PICKING TECHNIQUES

178

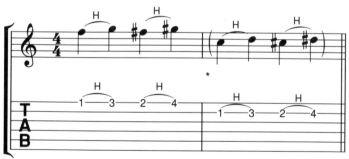

* Continue each exercise across all six strings

179

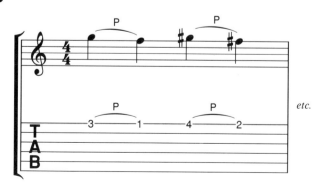

180

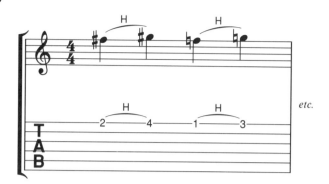

181

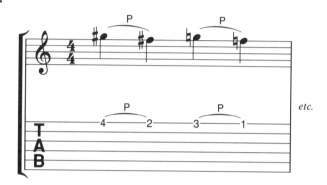

182

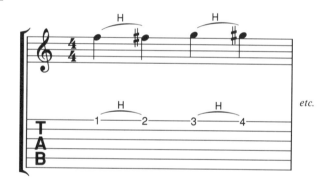

183

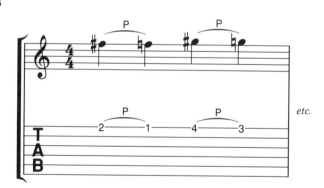

184

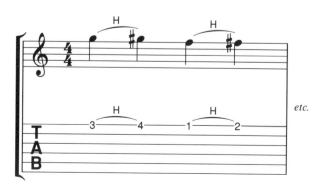

185

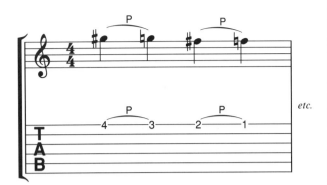

etc.

186

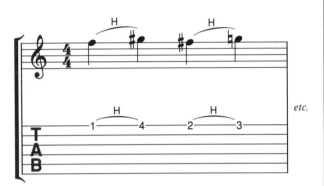

etc.

187

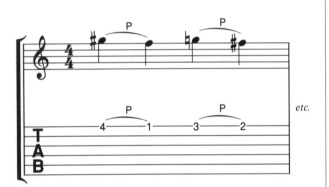

etc.

188

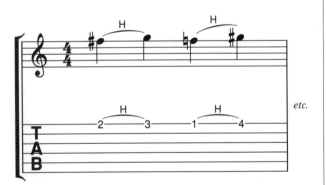

etc.

189

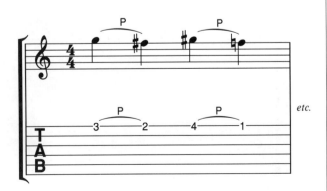

etc.

190

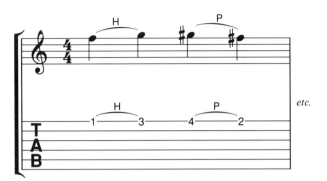

etc.

191

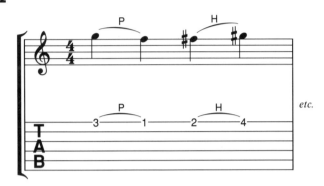

etc.

192

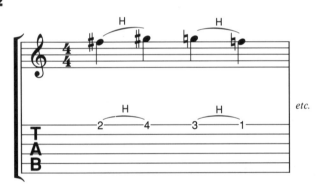

etc.

193

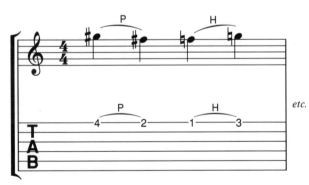

etc.

194

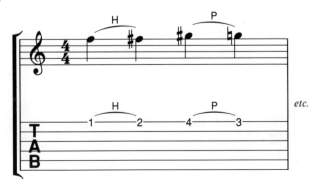

etc.

195

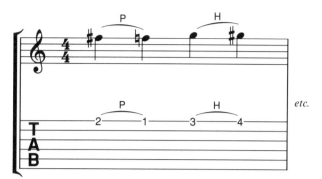

etc.

196

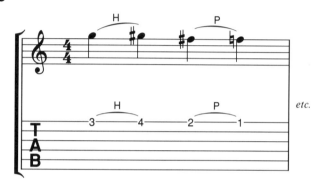

etc.

197

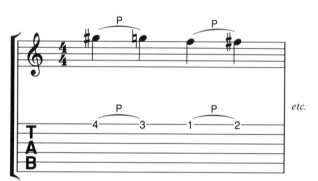

etc.

198

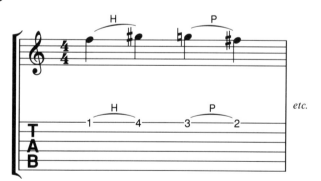

etc.

199

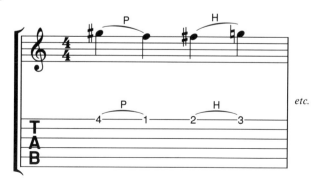

etc.

200

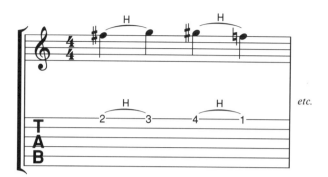

etc.

201

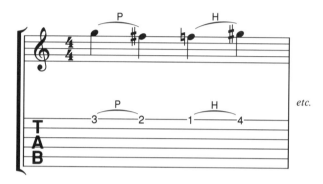

etc.

202

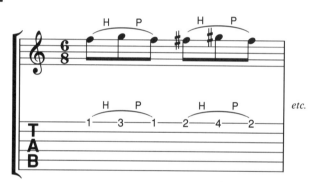

etc.

203

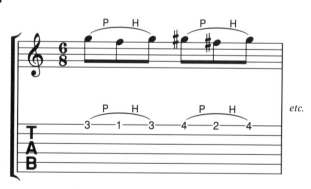

etc.

204

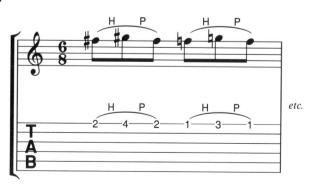

etc.

205

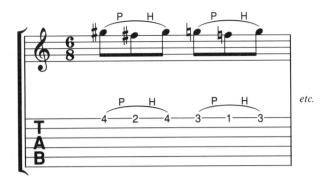

etc.

206

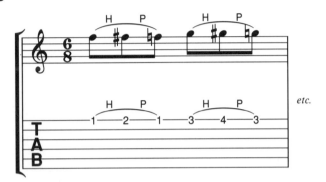

etc.

207

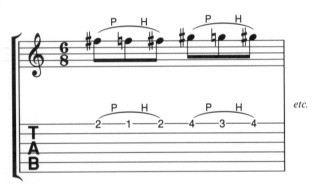

etc.

208

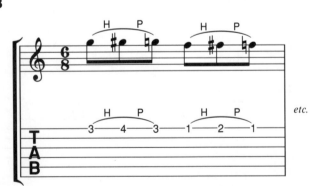

etc.

209

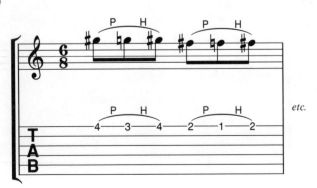

etc.

210

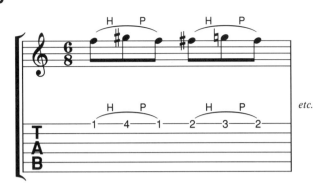

etc.

211

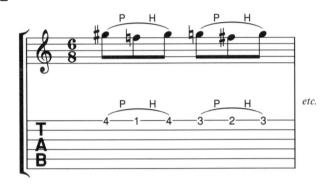

etc.

212

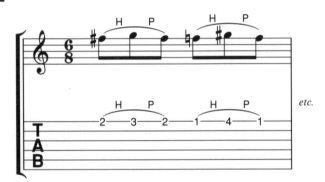

etc.

213

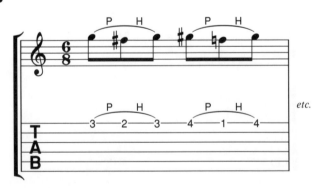

etc.

214

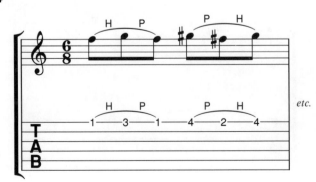

etc.

215

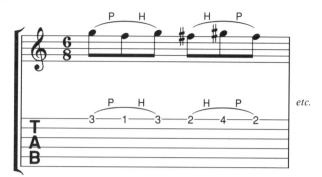

216

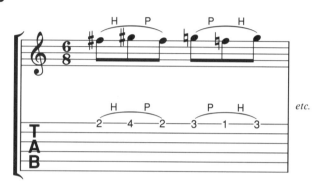

217

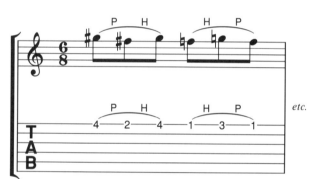

218

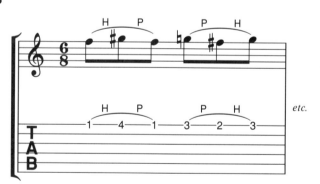

219

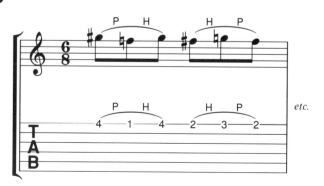

220

221

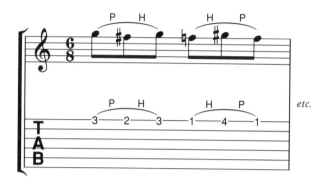

222

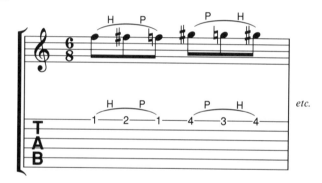

223

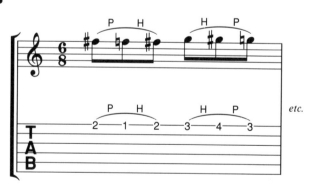

224

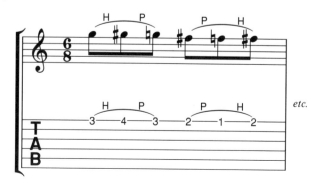

225

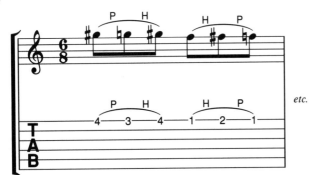

etc.

226

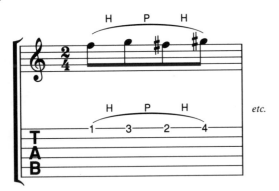

etc.

227

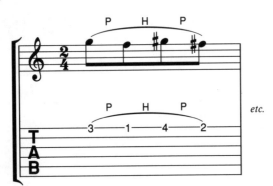

etc.

228

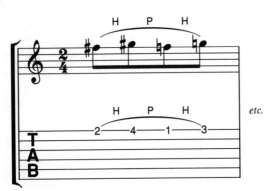

etc.

229

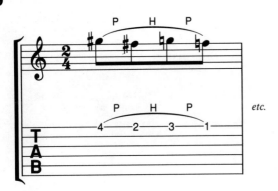

etc.

230

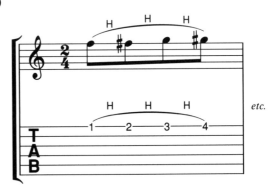

etc.

231

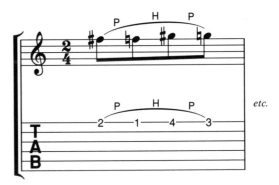

etc.

232

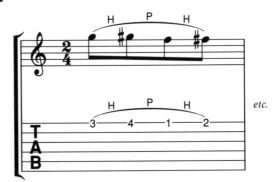

etc.

233

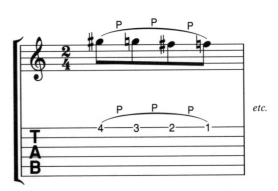

etc.

234

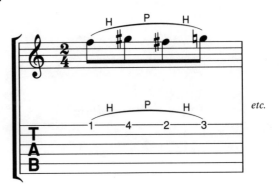

etc.

235

etc.

236

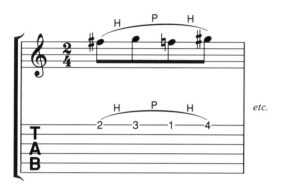

etc.

237

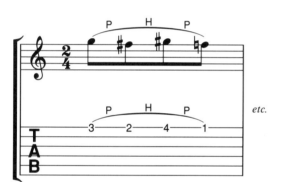

etc.

238

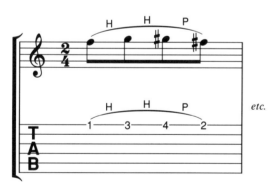

etc.

239

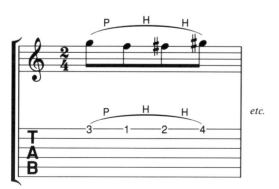

etc.

240

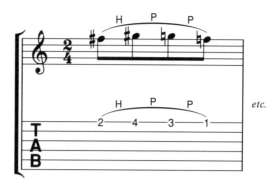

etc.

241

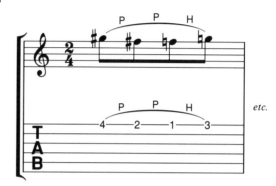

etc.

242

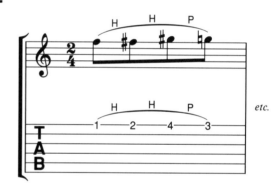

etc.

243

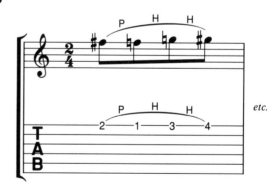

etc.

244

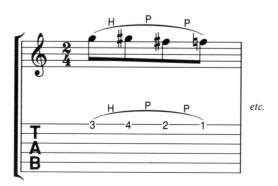

etc.

245

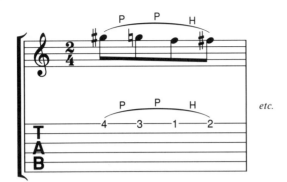

etc.

246

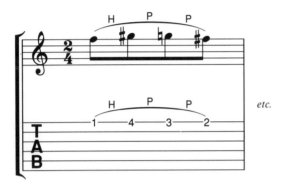

etc.

247

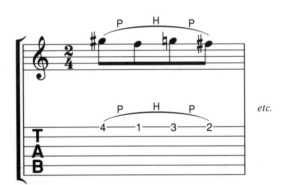

etc.

248

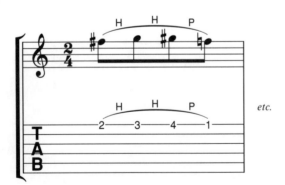

etc.

249

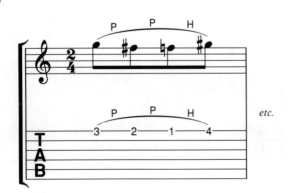

etc.

250

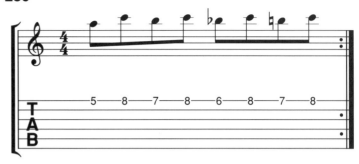

251

252

253

254

255

etc.

256

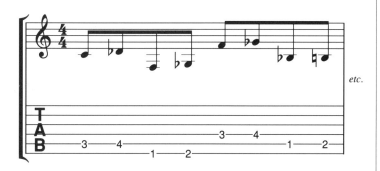

etc.

257

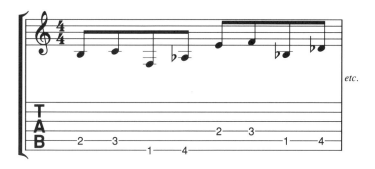

etc.

258 'Alternate picking' is probably the most obvious way of plucking the strings – you just alternate between downstrokes ⊓ and upstrokes V.

259 Some players almost exclusively use downstrokes. As with anything else to do with technique, if it works why change it?

260 Some players (Frank Gambale being one of the most famous) do a very great deal of their picking by raking the pick across a number of strings to produce arpeggio patterns. Gambale calls this 'sweep picking', although the basic idea has been around for a long time.

261 There is an approach which I've heard called 'economy picking'. This uses the pick to sweep across the strings wherever possible. The idea is to eliminate the need to 'jump' over a string to get to the next note in a scale type line (this happens a lot in alternate picking).

262 It's often useful to start a phrase on an upstroke if it means that you end up playing downstrokes on the beat.

263 If you use a plectrum, try playing the first solo of your gigs using only downstrokes. This will lock your right hand onto the string.

264 Note that the faster you play, the smaller your right hand movements must become. Very fast articulation requires that you make only very small movements.

265 Try not to arch your right wrist too much when you play, there's no need to stretch the muscle too far. If you feel pain in your wrist or arms, stop playing. You may be tensing up in order to push your technique – DON'T. The only way to get a really fluid technique is to practise, economise on movement and accept your current standard honestly.

266 If you play fingerstyle you'll have to spend a little time playing exercises which alternate adjacent right hand fingers. With a little practise you'll be able to liberate them from one another. If you're just starting out you'll probably have to decide whether to base your technique on the plectrum or the use of your right hand fingers. If you play classical guitar you'll definitely have to use your fingers. However, in most other styles there is generally room for both approaches.

267 If you normally use a plectrum but need to play arpeggio type patterns, you'll find it's pretty tricky playing these types of figures with a pick. Why don't you try holding the pick normally but also use the 2nd, 3rd and even the 4th right hand fingers to pick out the notes on the higher strings.

268 With this technique be careful that the notes played with the pick don't come out much louder than the others.

269 If you don't like the idea of using pick and fingers, try tucking the pick into your hand and hold it in place with your little finger. When you need it again you can just move it back into place.

270 If you use this technique, you will occasionally drop the pick. If you're doing a gig, you might try attaching a few plectrums to a microphone stand with adhesive tape.

271 Classical players will need to keep their nails well polished, but as metal strings tend to tear nails really badly, I would suggest you consider cutting your nails to avoid getting a scratchy tone with rough nail edges.

RIGHT HAND EXERCISES

272

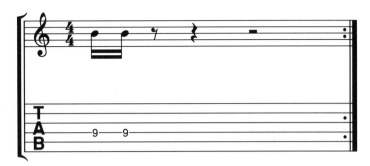

273

274

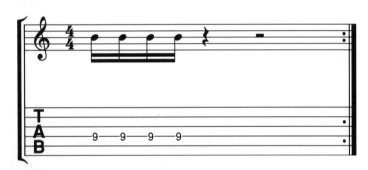

275

276

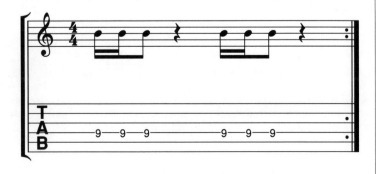

277

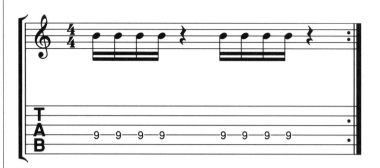

278

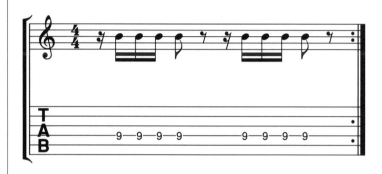

279

280

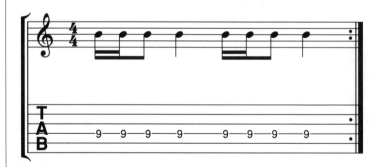

281

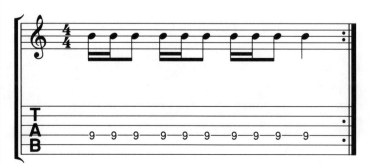

282

283

284

285

286

287

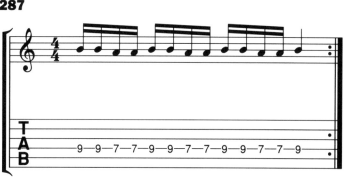

288

289 Remember to do your right hand drills on all the strings. They each have a different degree of resistance so you'll have to practise on each one to be equally fluid across them all.

RIGHT HAND TAPPING

290 Right hand tapping is a technique whereby right hand fingers are used to execute hammer-ons and pull-offs. The main benefit of this technique is that slurs can be executed beyond the reach of the left hand. To start tapping use only the right index or second finger.

291

(T = tap or hammer-on with your right hand)

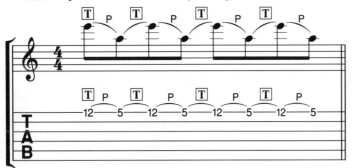

292 Here we move the same idea down the strings.

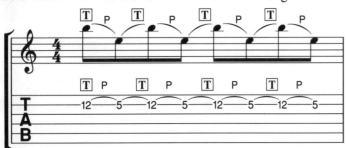

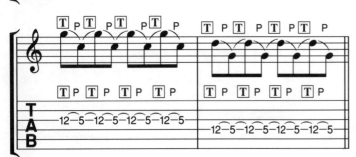

293

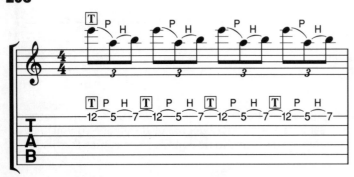

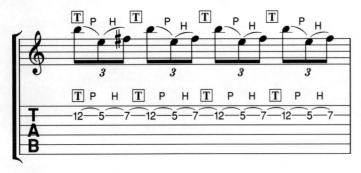

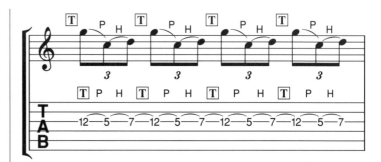

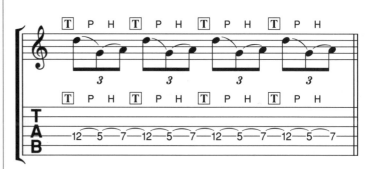

294

295

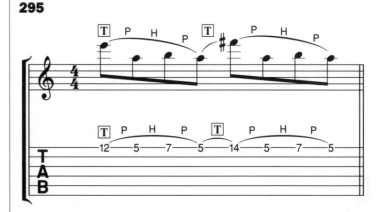

296 Arpeggios are one of the more useful sources of tapping material.

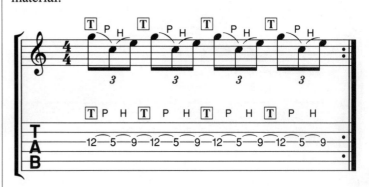

297

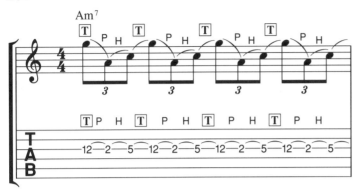

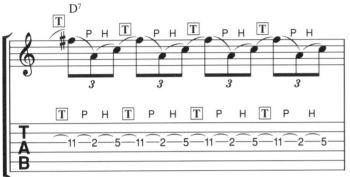

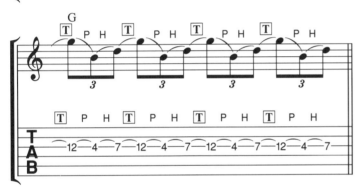

298

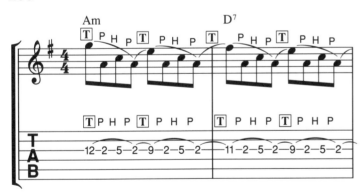

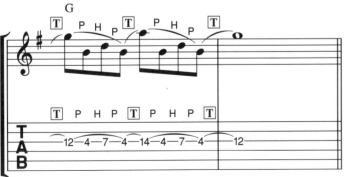

299

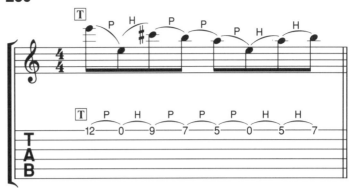

300 This line includes a slide executed by the right hand tapping finger.

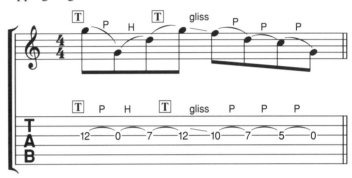

301 Here we bend from D up to E (3rd string) *then* tap at the twelfth fret. The string is already bent up a tone so the note sounded is A NOT G.

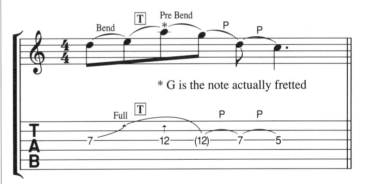

* G is the note actually fretted

302

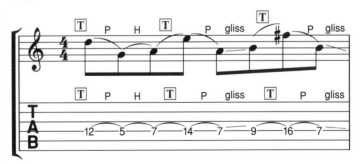

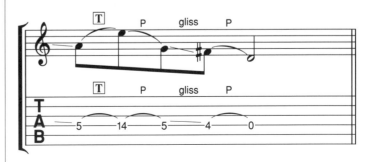

CLASSICAL GUITAR–
SPECIFIC RIGHT HAND TECHNIQUES

303 The term 'rest stroke' refers to the action of plucking a string where the right hand finger pushes through the plucked string and briefly comes to rest on the next lowest string.

304 The term 'free stroke' refers to the plucking action whereby the right hand finger moves through the string without coming into contact with the next lowest string.

305 The instruction 'Etouffé' means you are to execute a passage of music with the strings damped by the flesh of the right hand palm.

306 'Rasgueado' is a technique borrowed from flamenco. Clench your right hand fist then kick your fingers out one by one starting with the little finger. In this technique the outside of the finger makes contact with the string, not the inside, so the tone is quite abrasive.

307 'Tremolo' is a technique where a melodic line (generally quite a slow moving one) is played in quick repeated notes to create a shimmering sort of effect. The thumb generally picks out a bass note (but sometimes hits the repeated melody note) whilst in turn the ring, second and index fingers pick out the repeated top note.

308

309

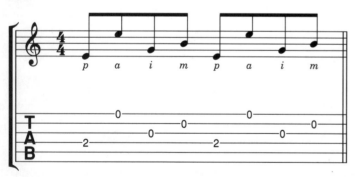

310

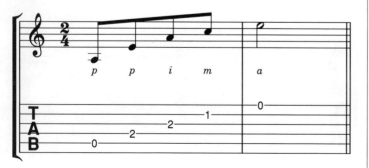

CARE OF THE HANDS

311 Don't practise the guitar with wet hands, you will almost certainly damage the first few layers of skin.

312 One of the best classical guitar players in the world told me not to wash my hands during the day OR to do the washing up. This might be a little unhygienic or unsociable for many people.

313 If you are forced to wet your hands, try to locate a hand dryer. An ordinary hairdryer will also do the trick. (A towel can leave your hands clammy).

314 Keep the fingernails of your left hand quite short – the most accurate way of fretting a note is with the tip of the finger. It's pretty painful if you trap a string under a fingernail.

315 Classical/fingerstyle players must keep their right hand nails well filed. The nail has a grain, just like a piece of wood – a tear on the edge of the nail will easily spread down the grain.

316 Ideally the edge of your right hand nails should be like glass. If it's not smooth you will DEFINITELY get a harsh scratchy tone.

317 To maintain a smooth edge you will need a nail file and some fine emery or sand paper (buy the finest grade possible).

318 To get a better edge to your nails, use a diamond cut nail file – they make for a cleaner finish.

319 For a perfect edge many leading classical players favour jeweller's polishing/finishing paper.

320 If you have particularly weak nails you can use false nails as a substitute or strengthen your own by applying a layer of clear nail varnish.

321 Plectrum players who use thicker picks may find that unused picks have a very scratchy sound. When you buy a new pick file the rough edge off – if the sound is still harsh use fine emery paper.

322 Thicker picks have a warmer sound than thin ones. For this reason jazz players tend to use a thicker pick than normal.

323 Rock players often use metal picks – they tend to give a sharp sound.

324 If you cut one of your fingertips you must be careful that contact with the strings doesn't open the wound further.

325 Minor scratches and cuts can be painted over with a plastic based false skin. When it's dry it gives protection that may well cover you for a practise session or even one set of a gig.

PRACTISE TIPS

326 It pays to make sure your practise space is conducive to good concentration – not too noisy, appropriate lighting, *etc.*

327 Be optimistic but, at the same time, realise where you stand. You have to be humble in order to take the best advantage of any learning opportunities.

B. B. King

328 Always try to make the best use of your practise time.

329 As soon as you feel yourself losing concentration, take a break. Don't feel you need to suffer for hours in order to achieve anything.

330 Don't practise what you can do, practise what you're having difficulty with.

331 Be patient – the benefits of any particular period of practise may only become obvious many months later.

332 Get in touch with your concentration span. If it's fifteen minutes, then respect that fact. Practise time will expand with experience.

333 Rather than starting the day with a rigorous technical workout why don't you try using this time (when you're most alert and possibly most creative) to improvise, compose or to seek a new viewpoint on the music you're working on.

334 If you're not enjoying playing, take some time off – it's not good to cement a mental association between music and pain/unhappiness.

335 However, there are ways of 'recharging your batteries'. If you're a little bored with your guitar, put a new set of strings on – it's surprising how much more sparky any guitar sounds with a new set of strings.

336 Record yourself playing – it will help you to get a picture of where you stand and you'll get a free lesson from the experience. Although you're very likely to be dissatisfied with what you hear, this process can set you off in some interesting directions.

337 You may occasionally feel that you're not improving. At these times try to remember the kind of things you were playing six months or a year ago – I'm sure you will have improved.

338 Don't forget to take breaks when you're practising, especially if the material you're studying is particularly challenging. Practising when you've lost concentration can be harmful to your progress.

339 Before you start to play any piece, it's crucial that you set the pulse going in your mind. Otherwise you'll spend a few seconds (or more) settling into a tempo.

340 It's worth finding the most appropriate tempo (speed) for any piece of music. The tempo can literally make or break the mood of a song.

341 The best way to improve your sense of pulse, and thereby make your playing much more convincing, is to use a metronome.

342 When you get a metronome, experiment with different tempos. Everyone has tempos which are comfortable and others which feel unnatural. Make sure you practise playing awkward tempos.

343 One slightly wacky tip is to set your metronome to an uncomfortable tempo and leave it running while you do some menial task, such as the washing up! The theory is that your subconscious will absorb the pulse.

344 Be sure to grimace at least occasionally – it will make the audience think you're doing something clever (maybe)!

345 Be aware of dynamics – this vital element of music gives light and shade to your playing. When you're rehearsing with a band, attention to detail in dynamics can really make your music come alive.

TUNINGS

346 Apart from the standard tuning there are a number of other tunings which have been commonly used. Blues players are the most adventurous group where tunings are concerned.

347 Open E tuning
1=E, 2=B, 3=G♯, 4=E, 5=B, 6=E.

348 Open D tuning
1=D, 2=A, 3=F♯, 4=D, 5=A, 6=D.

349 Open G tuning
1=D, 2=B, 3=G, 4=D, 5 =G, 6=D.

350 Try tuning your guitar a semitone flat
1=E♭, 2=B♭, 3=G♭, 4=D♭, 5=A♭, 6=E♭.

351 Try tuning your guitar a tone flat
1=D, 2=A, 3=F, 4=C, 5=G, 6=D.
Tips 350 and 351 give a fatter, looser sort of sound.

352 If you're using one of the last two tunings, you may find it necessary to use a heavier gauge of string to preserve the feel of the strings (and to enhance the tone).

353 One tuning which is very popular with folk guitarists is:
1=D, 2=A, 3=G, 4=D, 5=A, 6=D.

TRICKS AND DEVICES

354 If you're the sort of player who uses a lot of open position chords, you should get yourself a *capo*. This is a metal clamp which depresses all the strings in one fret space. It's particularly useful for accompanists where the singer wants to perform in a key for which open position chords are impossible.

355 If you're into right hand tapping (hammering on to notes with right hand fingers), it might be worth tying some soft material onto the strings at the nut to damp the ringing of sympathetic open strings.

356 Try adding a short delay effect to your sound when you solo. It helps to give more depth and body to the notes.

357 To give a smooth start to a note or chord, try fading in with a volume pedal or by rolling the volume control on your instrument – this is a useful device to give contrast – it makes the instrument sound less guitar-like and percussive in attack.

358 Artificial harmonics can be achieved by fretting a note normally with the left hand then lightly touching the string, twelve, seven or five frets higher with the right hand index finger. The third right hand finger is then used to pluck the string.

359 Artificial harmonics can also be played when you fret a note normally with the left hand but lightly touch the string with the flesh of your right hand while picking with a plectrum.

360 Use this technique when you haven't got the time to put the pick down to play an artificial harmonic.

361 Note that some artificial harmonics don't sound fully when certain pick-ups are used. This is because the magnetic pull of a pick-up will suppress the vibration of the string on various notes.

362 Because of this it's worth checking out which artificial harmonics come out cleanly with which pick-ups.

363 You can get a note to sustain on an electric guitar for a very long time by making the guitar feedback – you'll have to be fairly loud. Just point the instrument at the amp.

364 For extra drama try ending the feedback-sustained notes with a whammy bar dive.

RHYTHM

365 One of the most important steps you can take to improve your sense of rhythm is to get a metronome. The next step is to learn how to use it. I have some sort of drum pattern click going for most of my practise time.

366 The general bias leans towards pitch rather than rhythms. However, one of the most persuasive things about most great players is their sense of rhythm.

367 There's an old saying that if you play the wrong note in the right place (rhythmically speaking), it's half right, but if you play that note in the wrong place it's completely wrong.

368 To begin with you should aim to hit the note with the beat of the metronome. However, after a while you'll realise that there are many different ways to place the beat.

369 Try playing a very simple line at a moderate pace with your metronome going. Now slightly relax or hang back on the beat.

370 Try the same line at the same tempo but this time try to place the note very precisely on the beat. If another part of the band is playing slightly behind the beat, this kind of rhythmic delivery can be really powerful.

371 Now play the same line but try to actually push the metronome forward. This 'ahead of the beat' kind of feel can be very exciting, although it may be a little too aggressive for some styles.

372 A mature player might use all of these feels at different points. Drummers are often fun to check out. At a recent gig I saw jazz drummer Jack DeJohnette play – he's amazing because he can play with one limb playing behind the beat and another on top of the beat.

373 Of course if it's your solo, you're much freer to do what you want, but if you're just accompanying then you'd do well to try to lock in with the other players.

374 If you hear a rhythm you don't understand, try working it out. A lot of really ear-catching music gains its excitement from the rhythm more than the pitches used.

375 If you come across an interesting rhythm try to include it in your vocabulary and integrate it into your improvisation.

376 Some of the 'play-along' records (backing tracks which allow you to solo over a rhythm section such as Music Sales' 'Go Solo! ™' series) make it possible for you to experience playing with musicians without needing to leave your house.

377 There is a downside to this approach. Once you've started to be able to play along with recordings, it's time to get out there and find some other people to play with. It's much more fun to play in a band than just be a bedroom guitarist.

378 Some computer-based sequencing packages come with a selection of different quantising options (quantising is where the timing of recorded music can be uniformly adjusted to various degrees) which approximate a number of different feels. It's worthwhile checking this out if you already use this type of equipment.

Andy Summers

THE SURVIVORS' GUIDE TO GIGGING

AUDITIONS

379 Wear appropriate clothes to any audition. If you don't like the idea of a band's look, you probably won't enjoy playing with them.

380 Try to get your own gear to any audition or gig – you'll know how to get a good sound out of your own gear.

381 By the same token, if you're forced to use unfamiliar equipment, you must learn just to accept what's available and get on with it. (With a smile on your face.)

382 If you know you won't be able to use your amp maybe you can just use some of your own effects – at least they'll be familiar.

PLAYING WITH OTHER PEOPLE

383 When you're backing a singer, try to be aware of the melody notes. You want to support the melody, not get in the way.

384 When playing jazz, take care not to alter too many notes in any chord, unless you're pretty sure they'll fit in with the melody.

385 When you're asked to do a gig, find out how much space there is on-stage. There's no sense in taking a Marshall stack on a club gig where you've barely room to stand.

386 Whatever anyone else in the band does, show some respect for the audience – if they're not roaring with applause after the first song it's not necessarily their fault. We've all done gigs where the venue was just the wrong place for our kind of music.

387 Try to recruit people who enjoy the kind of music you play – guys who don't enjoy it will drag the whole project down.

388 When you're heading to a gig, take phone numbers for your band mates in case of emergencies.

Albert King

389 We must all learn to accept the current level of our skills. Being aware of our shortcomings is a blessing not a curse. Ignoring or not owning up to our weaknesses is just denying a chance to take another step forward.

390 If you end up playing in a band with players who aren't as keen as you are, try not to get annoyed, it's not realistic to assume that everyone should be as committed as yourself.

391 If you refer to our list of riffs and accompaniment figures, you'll notice that a lot of them are quite busy. However, when you come to play with a band you could strip your part down so that there's space for the rest of the band to do their bit.

392 If there's a keyboard player, or even a horn section, you'd be wise to just play a little figure to fit in between the other parts, maybe even just a few notes which repeat every four bars. Keep your ears open!

393 If you're playing in a jazz group with a keyboard player, you'll quickly realise that if you both play at the same time, it's a bit cluttered. In the big-band I play in, I came to an agreement with the piano player that I would accompany the tenor and baritone saxes and the trombones when they solo but the pianist would accompany the rest.

394 Always keep in check how loud you are compared to the other players – don't crank it up just because you think it sounds good!

REHEARSAL TECHNIQUES

395 Someone in the band must take charge of counting the tune in. In 4/4 the verbal count-in will be 'One, two, one-two-three-four'. (You'll see what I mean.)

396 In 3/4, the count-in will be '1-2-3, 2-2-3'.

397 If you have to count in a piece in any other time signature, for instance 5/4, it's best to count in with a couple of bars of that time signature.

398 If there's a tune where it's clear the different players are feeling different tempos, try a longer count in.

399 If you've got a strong (and well thought out) opinion as to what might make a piece sound better, then express it, otherwise don't bother. There's nothing more annoying than being bossed around by someone who just loves the sound of their own voice.

PREPARING FOR A PERFORMANCE

400 When preparing for a gig don't waste time on music you don't intend to play in public.

401 Make sure you devote the best part of your time to the music that needs it most.

402 If a piece is very ambitious it might be wiser (and gentler on the audience, ouch!) to leave it until a later date.

403 One way to minimise nerves on-stage is to make sure you're well prepared – this is where you'll realise the benefits of regular practise.

404 It's better to play one piece of music (however short) well than to play four or five badly.

405 If your band is inexperienced and a little nervous about a gig, try inviting a few friends along – at least you'll have someone rooting for you.

406 If you're hoping to get booked to do a gig a second time remember the promoter wants to see people come through the door. This is where the 'rentacrowd' of friends and relations will help your cause.

407 If you're a little nervous about a gig, don't worry, it's only natural. Even the most successful performers suffer from nerves. Nerves can actually be a real help to your concentration.

AT THE GIG

408 Give it your best shot on the gig – there's no time for indecision. Don't get into regretting mistakes – what's done is done.

409 Don't be shaken by what's going on around you, just concentrate on playing.

410 Don't struggle to acknowledge friends in the audience when you're trying to play. There will be plenty of time afterwards.

411 In the unlikely event that you bomb (or flop) on the gig, don't take a bad response too personally – try to be objective but be optimistic – if you get any strong response, at least you had enough presence to get a reaction – don't forget some of the greatest musicians had a lot of bad press early on in their careers.

412 Make sure you face the audience – if you don't it'll look like you've got something to hide.

413 If you're going to get into 'sitting in' on other people's gigs you must get used to the idea of just getting up, plugging in and playing. To make sure you get somewhere near the sound you're aiming for why not take a couple of effects pedals – they're quick to set up and easy to carry around.

RECORDING TIPS

414 When you're doing a recording, it's always worth experimenting with microphone placement. The smallest variations in the angle and distance from the speaker can make for huge differences in tone.

415 It might be worth your while to use more than one microphone, possibly one four or five inches from the speaker and another some feet away.

416 Experiment with putting a microphone to the rear of your amp, especially if it's an open backed cabinet.

417 When recording, it's often suggested that you record the guitar 'dry' (without effects) so that they can be added later. This is common practice in recording studios.

418 If you do record 'dry', make sure the engineer knows what kind of effects you would like to hear on your guitar.

419 If you are used to very long delays or lush reverbs, don't forget that the notes take a long time to end. This means that overdubs may not be so easy to do because the engineer will need to find longer gaps to avoid cutting a note in half.

420 Any serious studio will very probably have some really top class effects units – be flexible – just a bit of playing around on that Lexicon reverb could make all the difference to your sound.

421 If you're doing a demo, ask around to check out the reputation of any studio you're considering using. Studios which spend all day recording heavy metal bands may not be able to cut it when you're asking them to record a jazz outfit.

422 If you're doing your own recording you should think about which instruments are recorded in the same room as each other. You may find you want to record over the guitar solo but the previous solo can still be heard from the drum track recorded in the same room.

MUSICAL ATTITUDE

423 You can't be an expert in every field. Even the most successful session players only really get called to play two or three different styles of playing. These days there is a lot of room for individuality.

424 Always try to contribute the best you can, whatever the situation you'll always get something out of gigs if this is your attitude.

425 Realise people's strengths/weaknesses – calling a famous jazzer for a heavy metal gig might not always be a good move. It's no good getting frustrated with people when they're obviously not doing the kind of music they're good at.

426 You'll probably find yourself in situations where you join a new band and feel a little out of place. If people are a little quiet, don't worry – it's probably nothing to do with you. The bass player who doesn't say hello might have just crashed his car or could just be pre-occupied. Let's face it – all musicians are WEIRD so just do your bit – gradually people tend to open up.

427 Do you know how many guitar players it takes to change a light bulb – Ten. That's one to change the bulb and another nine to stand around saying 'I could have done that'. Think about it!!

428 Educate your ears and your hands will follow. There are a million good guitar players but really only a small number of originals.

429 Learning to play the guitar isn't easy but there will always be something to occupy you and entertain you. Long after you've seen all the latest videos or played the latest video games, the guitar will always be there as an outlet for your creativity, a release from the pressures of everyday life. Enjoy the guitar and your own special relationship with it.

ALL ABOUT SCALES

If you have problems finding the notes which fit a particular chord type you need some help. Here's a list of some of the basic scales and the types of chords they are naturally associated with. (We have given as an example chords based on C.)

430 The C major scale – naturally associated with the C major chord, C6 and C major 7th.

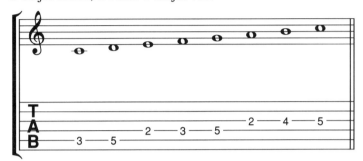

431 When improvising on the major scales, be careful to avoid emphasising the fourth degree – it's an ungainly sound.

432 The C7 scale (mixolydian-mode) – naturally associated with the C7 chord and its extensions (C9, C13, etc.).

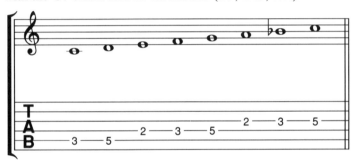

433 The C Natural minor scale – associated with Cm7.

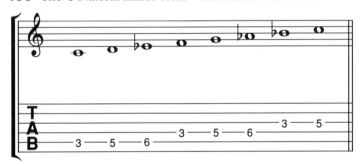

434 The C Dorian scale (Dorian mode) – very strongly associated with Cm7.

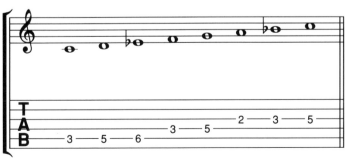

435 The C harmonic minor scale – used with Cm (with major 7th), G7♭9.

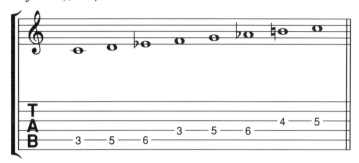

436 The C melodic minor scale. This scale can be used with Cm or Cm(maj7).

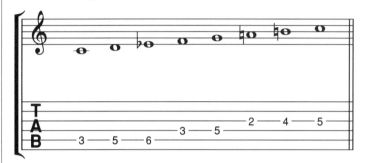

437 The Lydian scale (Lydian mode) fits the Cmaj7 ♯11.

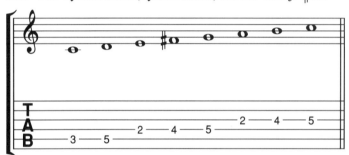

438 The Lydian dominant scale is perfect for the C7♯11 chord.

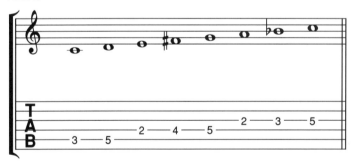

439 The C half diminished scale. This scale is commonly used on the II of a II-V-I in a minor key. (i.e. Cm7 in Cm7-F7-B♭)

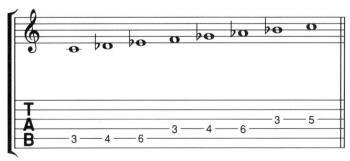

440 The C Blues scale. This scale with the minor 3rd and sharpened 11th, has a very characteristic sound. If the scale is new to you, be sparing in its use until you're more familiar with its colour. C Blues scales may be used with C major, C minor, Cm7 or C7 and various of its extensions including the C7♯9).

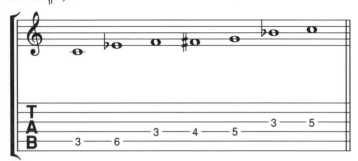

441 The C major Pentatonic scale. All the notes in this scale are good against C major.

442 The C minor Pentatonic scale.

443 Note that C major Pentatonic is the same as A minor Pentatonic starting on C. Therefore any patterns you work out for the major will also fit the minor scales.

444 Cultivate this kind of thinking – it will greatly expand how much use you get out of the musical material stored in your memory.

445 Pentatonic scales have a great many uses. The two mentioned above if used over C major and C minor respectively are very consonant, if a little obvious. Jazz artists such as John Coltrane, McCoy Tyner and Chick Corea expanded the scales' use by using them over other chords to imply more dissonant sounds. By using a smaller part (the Pentatonic scale) of a whole scale your lines will sound more concise, even more specific.

446 The C jazz dominant scale (the 'bebop scale'). This scale was designed to fit over the C7 and Gm7 chords. The major 7th is used as a passing note to fill in the gap between the root and flattened 7th degrees of the chord.

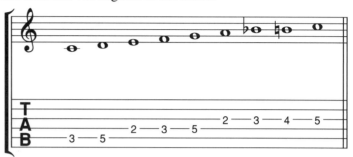

447 C whole tone scale. This scale fits C7♯11.

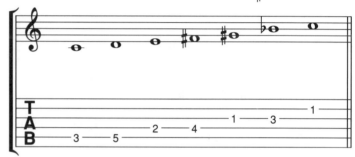

448 C diminished (often called 'half step/whole step diminished'). This scale forms the basis for a wealth of great musical lines. It's probably most popular with jazz musicians. Use this scale over C7 but listen to the altered notes of the scale.

449 C altered scale. This scale fits C7 altered (i.e. C7♯9, C7♯5♯9, C7♭9, C7♯5♭9, etc.). Note the similarity of this scale to the whole tone scale.

450 The Phrygian mode. This scale is often credited with a Spanish colour.

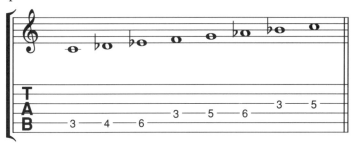

451 The chromatic scale.

452 The Lydian augmented scale. This scale fits Cmaj7♯5.

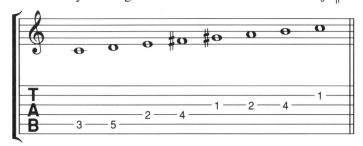

453 The most powerful way to motivate yourself to explore any new scale is to find a tune which features the scale.

454 There are a number of 'play-along' books available which give you the backing track and chords. This is a fun way of practising your scales, and learning to improvise.

DEMONSTRATIONS FOR EACH SCALE

455 C Major

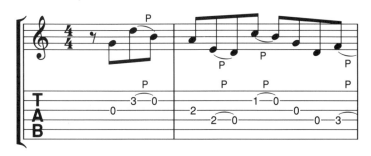

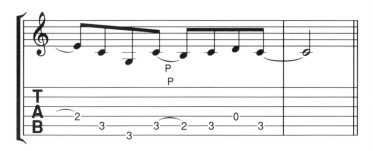

456 C Mixolydian (C7 Scale)

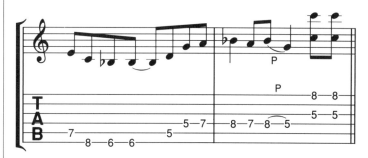

457 C Natural Minor

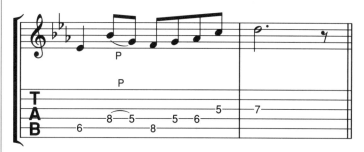

458 C Dorian

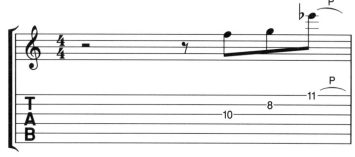

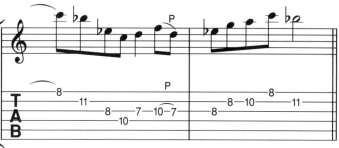

459 C Harmonic Minor

460 C Melodic Minor

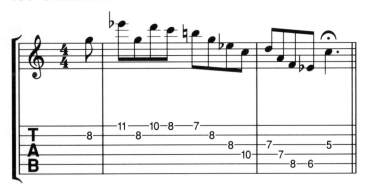

461 C Lydian

462 C Lydian Dominant

463 C Half Diminished

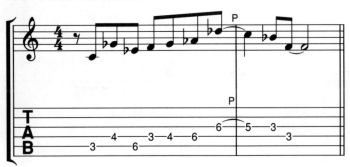

464 C Blues

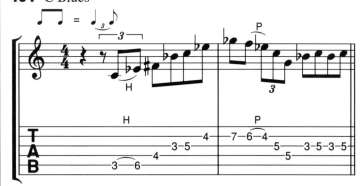

465 C Major Pentatonic

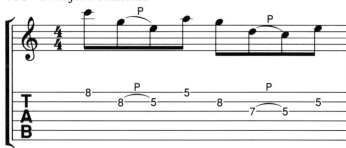

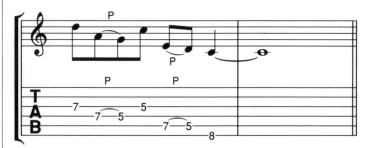

466 C Minor Pentatonic

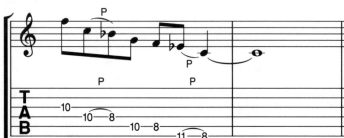

467 C Jazz Dominant

468 C Whole Tone

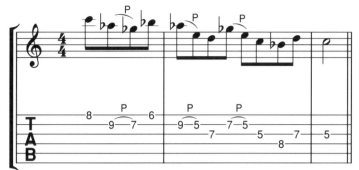

469 C Diminished (starting with half step)

470 C Altered

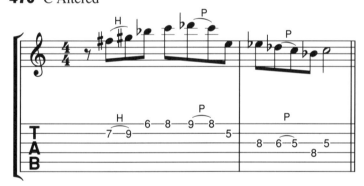

471 C Phrygian

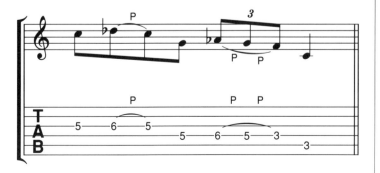

472 C Lydian Augmented

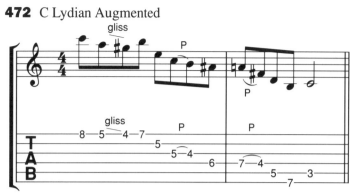

473 G♭ Major Pentatonic over C7 gives an altered scale sound.

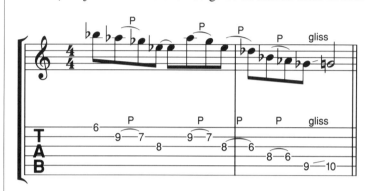

PRACTISE YOUR SCALES OVER THESE BACKING VAMPS

474 C Major

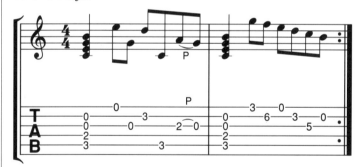

475 More C Major

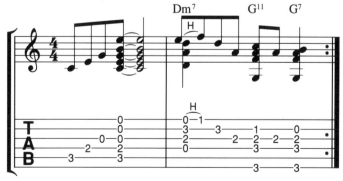

476 C7

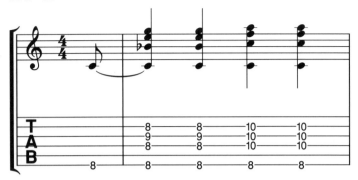

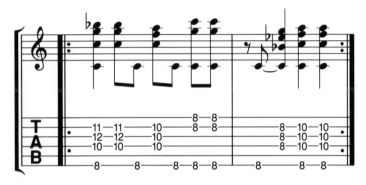

477 C Natural Minor

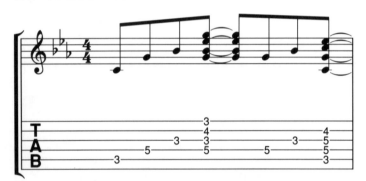

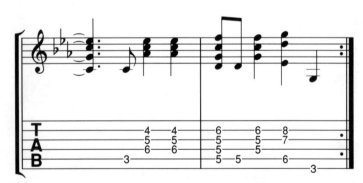

478 C Harmonic Minor

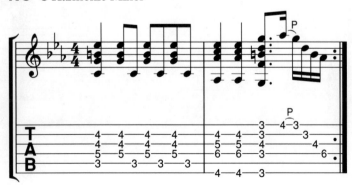

479 C Dorian

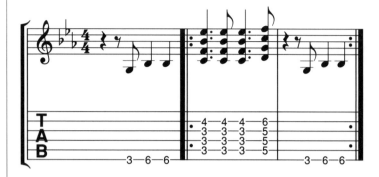

480 C Lydian

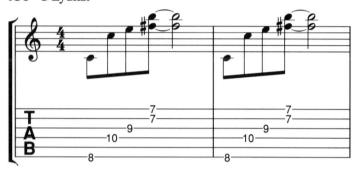

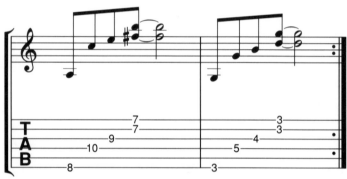

481 C Lydian Dominant

482 C Half Diminished

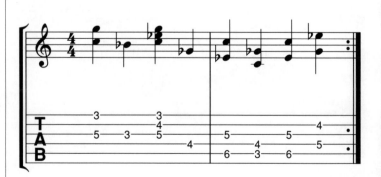

483 C Blues Scale (Blues scale over C7)

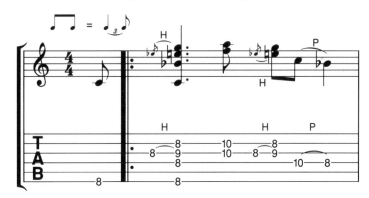

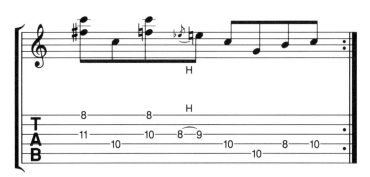

484 C Blues Scale

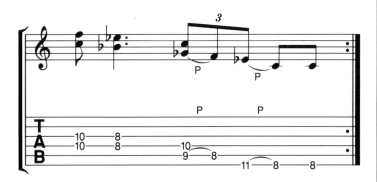

485 C Major Pentatonic – try it over Vamps 1, 2, 3, 7 or 8.

486 C Minor Pentatonic – try it over Vamps 4, 6 or 8.

487 C Jazz Dominant – 'The Bebop Scale' – use it over Vamps 3 and 10.

488 C Whole Tone

489 C Diminished (starting with a half step or semitone).

490 C Altered

491 Phrygian

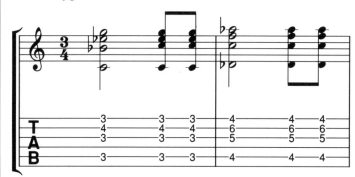

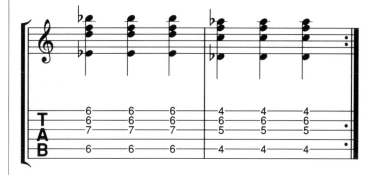

492 E Phrygian (E, F, G, A, B, C, D)

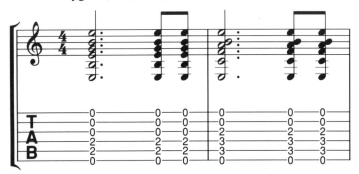

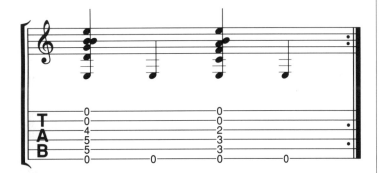

493 C Lydian Augmented (C, D, E, F♯, G♯, A, B)

494 Try this vamp with G♭ Major Pentatonic over C7.

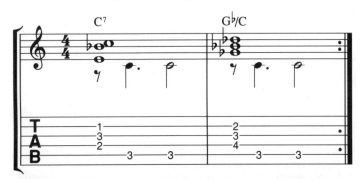

John McLaughlin

LET'S TALK ABOUT IMPROVISATION

495 When you're beginning your exploration of improvisation, start small and just play around with some ideas.

496 The easiest way to begin improvising is to start by playing a melody that you already know and then just embellish the notes of the melody.

497 Start leaving notes out of this original borrowed melody.

498 What does it sound like if you start substituting some of your own notes for those in the original?

499 If you persist with this approach, pretty soon you're hardly referring to the original at all. Easy isn't it!

500 Try playing along with your favourite records – it'll help your sense of rhythmic pulse and improve your ear.

501 If you're checking out a new scale or chord type make a backing track of the appropriate chord and practise playing along with it. By the time you come to use this material with other musicians it will be familiar ground.

502 Try playing your scales along one string. If you work on this approach you'll be able to make sense of the fretboard wherever your fingers are on it.

503 Take any particular scale and figure out where the notes are along one string. Now try to improvise on the scale limiting yourself to that one string. You could play along with one of our suggested vamps.

504 Now take the scale, pick a pair of adjacent strings and improvise limiting yourself to those two strings.

505 Try the above but with a pair of strings which are not adjacent. You can come up with some pretty wild stuff in this way. Listen to John Scofield for some great wide interval lines.

506 Now try the same process on three strings.

'MAKING THE CHANGES'

507 If you're having problems making sense of a particular chord progression, there's a simple method to start you off on the right track.

　1. Go through the chords playing up the basic triad for each one…

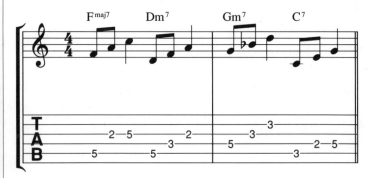

508 2. Go through the chords playing up to the 7th degree of the scale.

509 3. Go through the chords playing the 1st, 2nd, 3rd and 5th degrees of each chord.

510 4. Now reverse the pattern (5th, 3rd, 2nd, 1st).

511 5. Now take another step up in the chords – play the 3rd, 4th, 5th and 7th degrees of each chord.

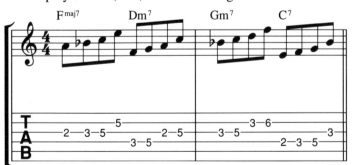

512 6. Next reverse that shape (7th, 5th, 4th, 3rd).

513 7. Try going even higher up the chords. Play the 5th, 6th, 7th and 9th degrees of each chord.

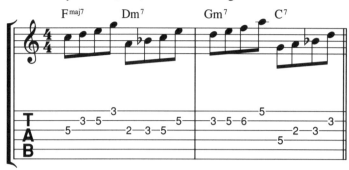

514 8. Reverse this pattern (9th, 7th, 6th and 5th).

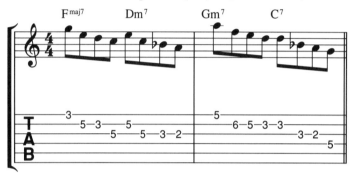

515 All of this might sound mechanical but notice the notes all sound right for each chord. By maintaining this exercise, you will be able to hear the colour of each chord much more clearly.

516 Next you should experiment, albeit slowly, with linking the chord tones together – start on one chord and find the nearest note contained in the next. Notice how much more clear the progression between the chords becomes.

517 If you find a lick or pattern that appeals to you, try transposing it into all the other 11 keys. On the guitar this often means just shifting the finger shape up or down the fingerboard. If this seems a little daunting just think of the plight of a piano player or saxophonist – the same pattern is fingered quite differently from key to key.

518 Get into the habit of isolating phrases and trying to work out where they would fit in the pieces you're playing.

519 If you're checking out a new artist or style of music try working some of it out for yourself from the recording.

520 You'll find that transcribing (working out a pattern) is one of the most valuable things you can do to add to your vocabulary. It will really help your ear. Even though transcription books can be very helpful, the stuff that you worked out yourself will always have more meaning to you. You'll be much less likely to forget this material.

521 Have faith that your transcribing skill will improve. Take it in small doses at first and, above all, enjoy it!

522 When you get 'stuck' with a difficult phrase, listen to it on a different machine. Sometimes you'll hear more of what you want to hear on a cheap machine than on your treasured hi-fi.

523 Try listening to things at radically different volumes, generally it's more effective to turn the volume down but try all the options (neighbours permitting).

524 You'll really punish your tape deck and CD player by regularly transcribing. I often use a really cheap tape recorder to get the outline of a piece but move onto my more expensive gear to get the details.

525 If you do have a transcription of one of your favourite pieces but it looks rather hard to play, try breaking it down into very small fragments. Gradually, you'll get closer and closer.

526 Sometimes to make an idea playable you might have to simplify it. This is often the case with music played on another instrument where some things are easier to execute than on the guitar, e.g. the saxophone.

527 As soon as you start this process, you're already personalising the material at hand.

528 Personalising material you've transcribed will really come into its own when you start improvising with them.

VOICINGS

529 C major.

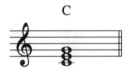
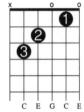

530 C6.

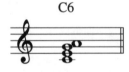
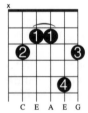

531 C major 7.

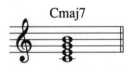
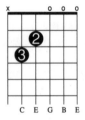

532 Cadd9.

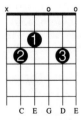

533 Csus2.

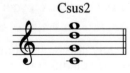

534 C7.

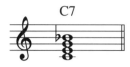

535 C minor.

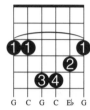

536 C minor 7.

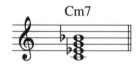
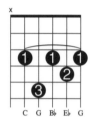

537 When voicing a Minor 7th chord which moves to a Dominant 7th chord a fourth higher, avoid hanging onto the sixth degree – it makes it sound too much like the Dominant chord.

538 C Minor 6th.

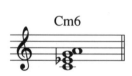

539 Note the similarity between C6 and Am7 (they are built from the same notes C, E, G, A). Voicings learned under the name of one can obviously be substituted for the other.

540 Cm7♭5. This chord is often used as a II chord leading to a Dominant 7th (V) when approaching a Minor chord (I).

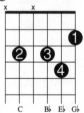

541 Note that Cm7♭5 is built from the same notes as E♭ minor 6th (C, E♭, G♭, B♭).

542 C7sus4.

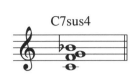 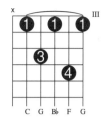

543 C7♯9. This chord is sometimes referred to as the 'Jimi Hendrix chord'.

544 C7♭9.

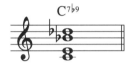 

545 C7♭13.

546 This last chord is particularly useful when the next chord is F minor. The flattened thirteenth on C7 is the minor third of F. It seems a more fitting note than the natural thirteenth – A.

547 C7♯11.

 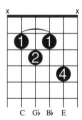

548 Cdim.

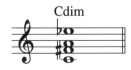 

549 C5 – primarily a heavy rock device – a bare root and fifth.

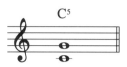 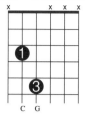

550 There are two ways to approach chords.
1. Learn a few voicings for each chord and stick to them,

or

2. Learn the way in which the chords are constructed.

551 If you have a limited amount of time and energy available to spend with your guitar, option 1 may be the better method for you.

552 If you have more time, option 2 will allow you to find a far greater number of ways to play any chord.

553 Although basic chord shapes all have the root of the chord at the bottom, this note is not always needed in your voicing if you are playing with bass.

SELECTING CHORD VOICINGS

MAJOR 7th CHORD VOICINGS

554 Cmaj7.

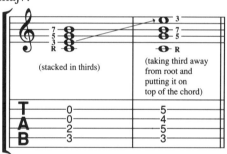

555 Cmaj7.

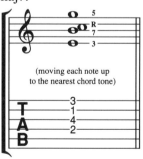

556 Cmaj7.

557 Cmaj7.

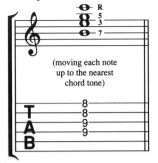

(moving each note
up to the nearest
chord tone)

558 Cmaj7.

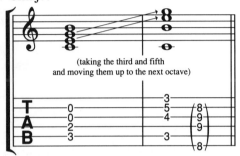

(taking the third and fifth
and moving them up to the next octave)

559 Cmaj7.

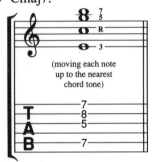

(moving each note
up to the nearest
chord tone)

560 Cmaj7.

(moving each note
up to the nearest
chord tone)

561 Cmaj7.

(moving each note
up to the nearest
chord tone)

DOMINANT 7th CHORD VOICINGS

562 C7

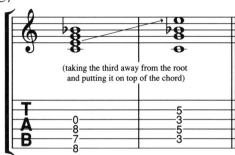

(taking the third away from the root
and putting it on top of the chord)

563 C7

(moving each note
up to the nearest
chord tone)

564 C7

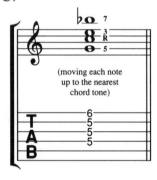

(moving each note
up to the nearest
chord tone)

565 C7

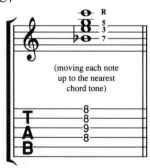

(moving each note
up to the nearest
chord tone)

566 C7

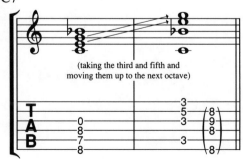

(taking the third and fifth and
moving them up to the next octave)

567 C7

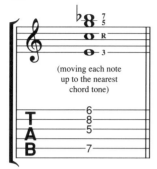

(moving each note
up to the nearest
chord tone)

568 C7

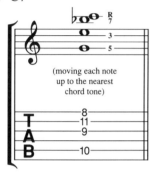

(moving each note
up to the nearest
chord tone)

569 C7

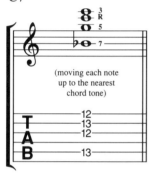

(moving each note
up to the nearest
chord tone)

MINOR 7th CHORD VOICINGS

570 Cm7

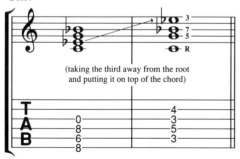

(taking the third away from the root
and putting it on top of the chord)

571 Cm7

(moving each note
up to the nearest
chord tone)

572 Cm7

(moving each note
up to the nearest
chord tone)

573 Cm7

(moving each note
up to the nearest
chord tone)

574 Cm7

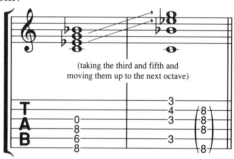

(taking the third and fifth and
moving them up to the next octave)

575 Cm7

(moving each note
up to the nearest
chord tone)

576 Cm7

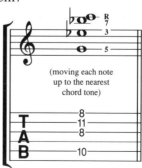

(moving each note
up to the nearest
chord tone)

577 Cm7

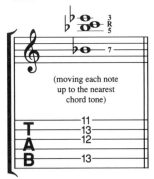

(moving each note up to the nearest chord tone)

578 As accompanists we really need to consider the kind of harmonic texture we're supplying – is it really appropriate?

579 Remember that sometimes a lighter texture will be much more effective. The tone of the guitar can be so expressive that it doesn't need to fill all the gaps to create an atmosphere.

580 You could keep the texture thin, holding fire until the most triumphant chorus where you might decide to 'rock out'.

581 A thick texture can be created by constantly playing six-string chords.

582 A medium texture can be created by the guitar playing chords with some space between them, leaving room for the vocal and the rest of the rhythm section.

583 If you're going for a sparse texture, leave a lot of space and use a lot of single lines and double stops – U2's guitarist 'The Edge' is a great exponent of open textures.

584 As you get used to the people you're playing with you'll find you develop a feeling for the kinds of scales and phrases they tend to go for. As this happens you'll find more and more appropriate ways of accompanying them.

EXPANDING THE BASIC CHORDS

585 When you see a basic C major chord you can add the 6th or 9th to give a slightly different edge to the sound.

586 To make a major chord brighter you can try adding the 9th degree of the scale on top. (C becomes C add 9). The Police often used this chord (check out 'Every Breath You Take').

587 In songs where there is lot of time spent on the tonic 7th chord, you might try a 7#9 chord. Check it will fit in with the melody. This is a funky/bluesy kind of sound.

588 In heavy metal style songs you may even find yourself slimming the chords down to the bare root and fifth, at least for some part of rockier tunes.

589 In funk tunes where a minor 7th type chord is held for a long period try alternating between the minor 7th and minor 6th. This sounds best if you keep the minor 7th to minor 6th movement on the top line of your voicing. Check out some James Brown records.

590 If there's a dominant seventh (a V7 chord) you can precede it with a minor 7th chord a fifth higher. This makes a II-V progression and can add a little more movement to a chord progression.

591 As always you need to keep your ears open to decide whether the chords fit in with the style of music you're playing.

592

If you have this:

you could play:

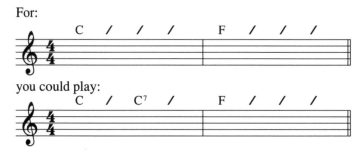

593 Or you could play:

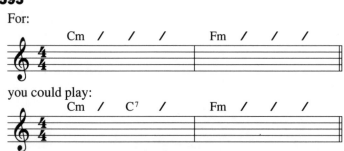

594 If a chord moves to another a fifth below you can often make the first chord a dominant 7th.

For:

you could play:

595

For:

you could play:

596 For the last example remember that the C7 chord will sound best with a flattened 13th (Ab) as this notes signals we're going to Fm NOT F major.

597 The same rule can apply to the II-V progression.

For:

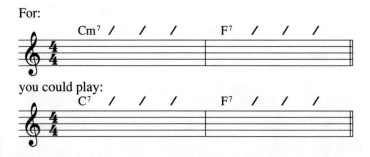

you could play:

Thus we're taking advantage of the fact that the Cm moves down a fifth to slot in as a dominant 7th resolving temporarily on F7, which in turn would resolve to Bb. This device is called a 'secondary dominant'.

598 Jazz musicians often use altered dominant 7ths.

For:

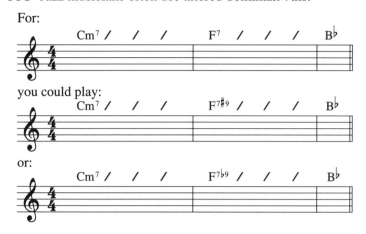

you could play:

or:

Other altered extensions you could try are the sharpened 11th (raised 4th degree), the flattened thirteenth or even the 7th with added 11th degree.

599 Normally when the 11th is present in a 7th chord the third is omitted.

600

For:

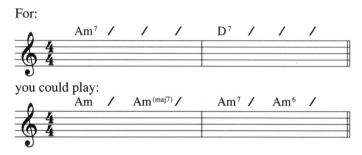

you could play:

601 While we're talking jazz, it's often possible (melody permitting) to use a dominant 7th with sharpened 9th for the tonic chord. Jazz pianist Bill Evans plays this type of chord at the opening of the beautiful standard 'When I Fall In Love'. This is also a favourite Jimi Hendrix sound (check out 'Purple Haze').

LEARNING TO LISTEN

602 The ability to discern intervals and chords directly relates to the speed at which you will pick up new music.

603 Don't get discouraged if you find it difficult hearing what's going on in a piece of music. A large amount of pitch recognition is to do with familiarity.

604 Be patient – when you can recognise the interval between two notes in a melody, the next step is to find the interval between the next two. Pretty soon you'll be hearing the connection between larger groups of notes. Have faith.

605 Practise the following exercises when you're going about your daily business – walking down the road, lying in the bath, *etc., etc*.

606 In The Bleak Mid Winter (Minor 2nd)

607 Alouette (Major 2nd)

608 Oh Susanna (Minor 3rd)

609 Humpty Dumpty (Major 3rd)

610 The Eensy Weensy Spider (Perfect 4th)

611 Maria (West Side Story) (Augmented 4th)

612 Twinkle, Twinkle Little Star (Perfect 5th)

613 Old King Cole (Minor 6th)

614 My Bonnie Lies Over The Ocean (Major 6th)

615 Somewhere (West Side Story) (Minor 7th)

616 Over The Rainbow (Major 7th)

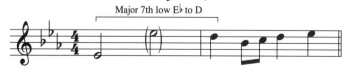

617 Over The Rainbow (Octave)

618 Try to find a friend of roughly the same standard and test each other on aural recognition.

619 Listen to the different chords looking for a mental/emotional association with each one. Some will sound 'sweeter' than others, they may even suggest a particular picture to you.

620 A friend of mine always calls diminished chords 'cartoon chords' because he associates them with the very colourful depictions of evil characters used for cartoon music scores. These kinds of associations are very useful in identifying chords.

621 The very best way to get your ears together is to learn songs. In no time you'll have the sound of the chords of your favourite tunes ringing around your head.

622 Remember that in any kind of music there are certain harmonic formulas or chord progressions which come up time and time again.

623 Playing along with records will definitely help. Another helpful trick is to record an accompaniment to some tunes you're thinking of learning.

624 Try making a tape of four or five new tunes. Leave the tape for a few days and when you come back to it see how much you can remember and how much you can figure out without the music.

625 It's a great thrill to be able to work out the tune to a new piece.

INTERVALS

626 If you spend a lot of time working on your own, it's worth taping longish sequences of intervals/chords to test yourself. If you make a few different tapes, you can start the tape in different places so that your memory doesn't help you cheat.

627 Start by working on identifying major and minor 2nds.

628 Move on to major and minor 3rds.

629 When you feel you're getting the colour of these intervals, mix them all up (either by taping them or getting a friend to test you).

630 Now add in the 4ths, including the augmented 4th.

631 The 5ths come next.

632 Now the major 6th and minor 6th.

633 Now the major 7th and flattened 7th.

634 Notice that certain intervals have something of a similar sound. For instance the perfect 4th/perfect 5th and the minor third/major 6th. This is because each of these pairs is the other one turned upside down. They are 'inversions' of each other.

CHORDS

635 First you should just play straight major and minor chords until you can immediately tell the difference. The major is brighter than the minor.

636 Then pick the dominant 7th. Try to differentiate between this and the straight major. I think the 7th degree of this chord makes it more soulful, more bluesy than the major. Play these chords randomly until you feel the distinct colour of each.

637 Play these chords, firstly with the 6th, then 5th and 4th strings (i.e. play a given chord in different positions on the neck).

638 Now add the major 7th and minor 7th chords to the cauldron.

639 Add the diminished and augmented chords. They each have a very individual sound.

640 Now try the half diminished chord. Play it on its own until you start to hear its character, then mix it up with the others.

641 If it's a problem just picking this, or any other chord type out of the whole range of chords (you're not alone!), try just limiting the options to three or four chord types.

642 Eventually you'll get to the point where you can start work on identifying the dominant 7th chords with extensions (9th, 11th, 13th), even altered extensions. Try to find tunes where the melodies feature these extended notes of the 7th chord.

643 Don't spend so much time on ear training that it becomes a chore.

Jimmy Page

ROCK RIFFS

644

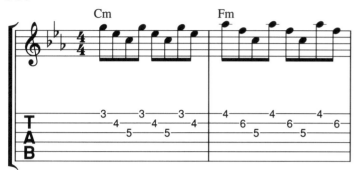

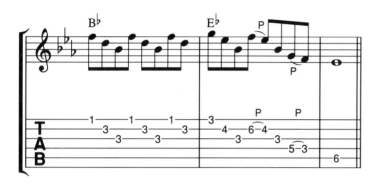

645

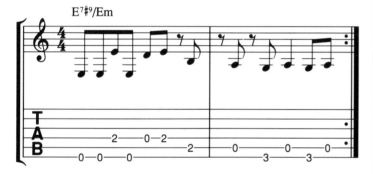

646

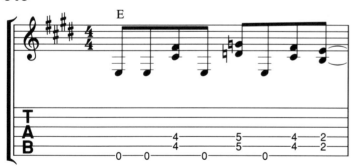

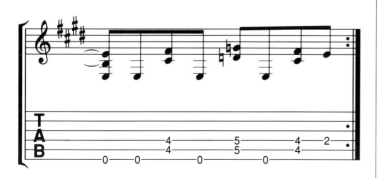

647

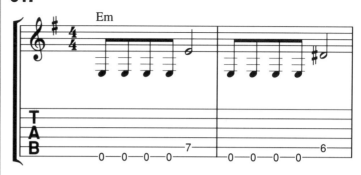

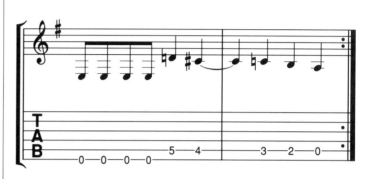

648

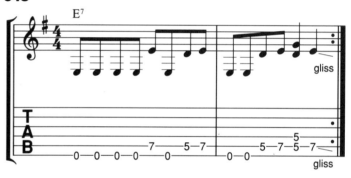

649

650

651

652

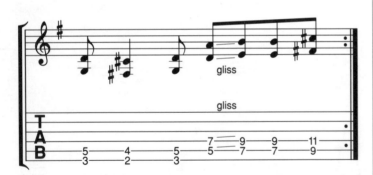

ROCK AND RHYTHM

653

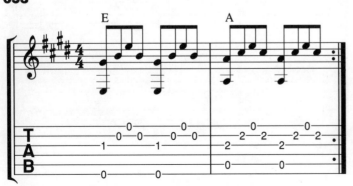

654

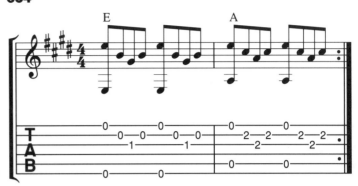

655

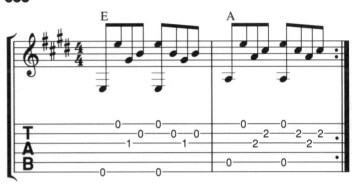

656

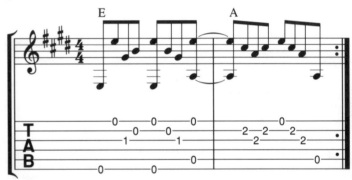

657

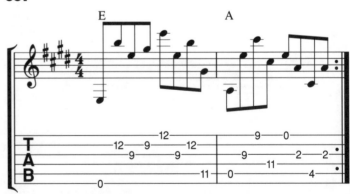

658

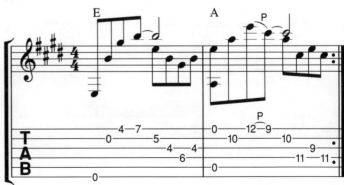

659

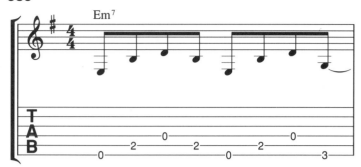

660

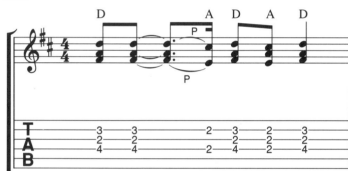

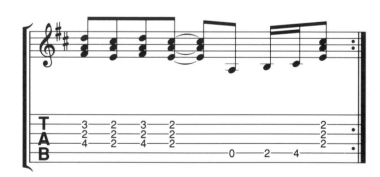

661

662

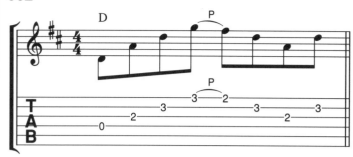

663

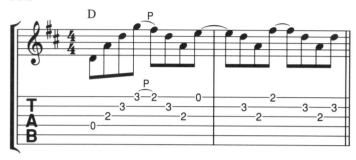

664 Very Jimi Hendrix!

665

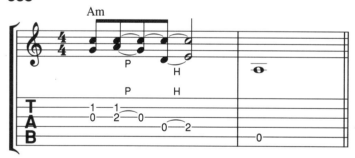

666

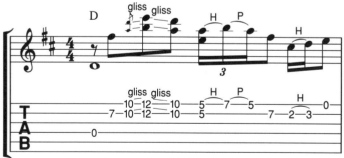

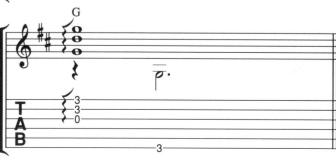

676

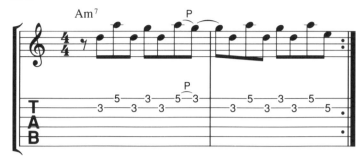

677

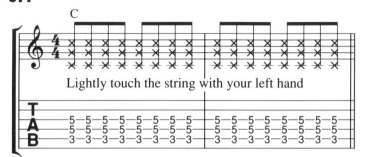

Lightly touch the string with your left hand

678

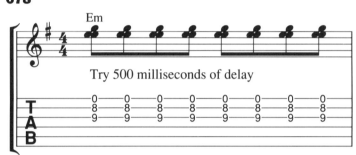

Try 500 milliseconds of delay

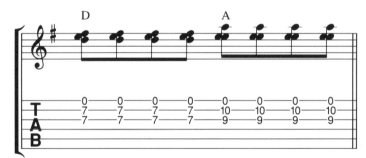

679

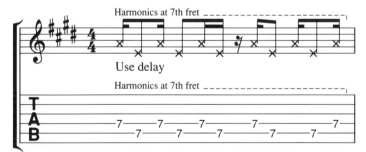

Use delay

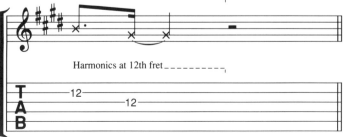

680

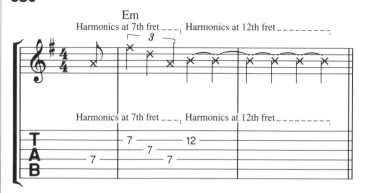

681

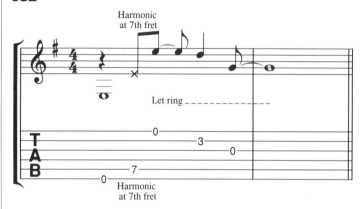

The Edge (U2)

TAKING THE LEAD

682

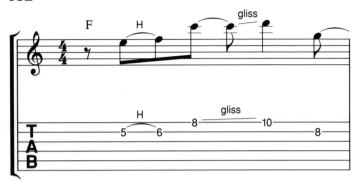

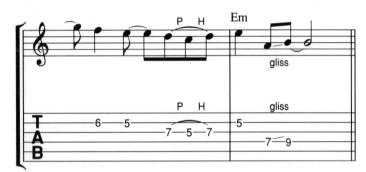

683

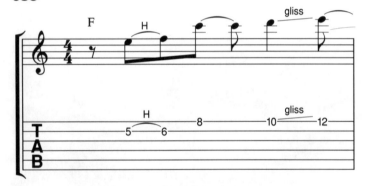

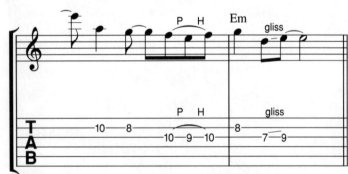

684

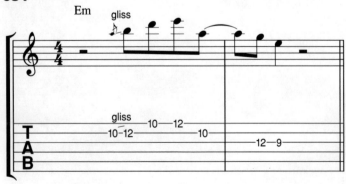

685

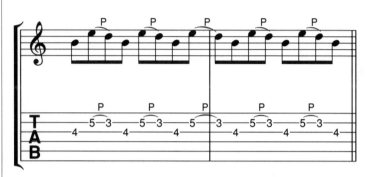

686

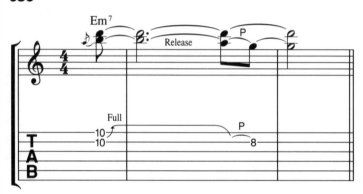

687

688

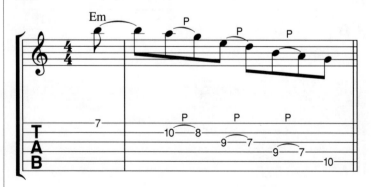

689

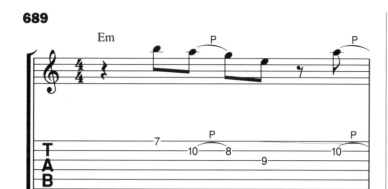

690

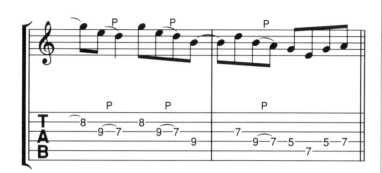

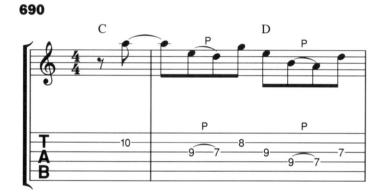

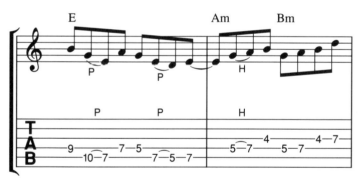

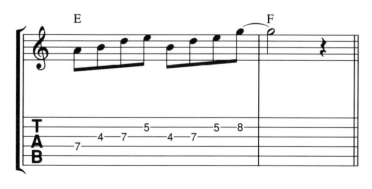

691

692

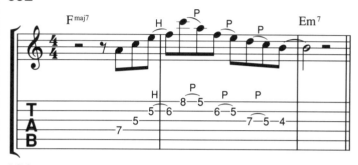

693

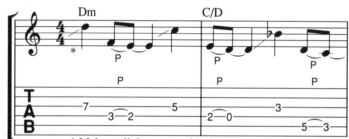

* Make a slight scoop with the
whammy bar at the start of the note

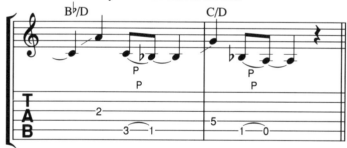

694

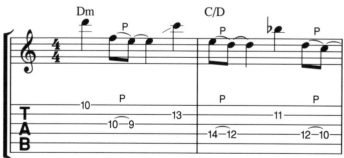

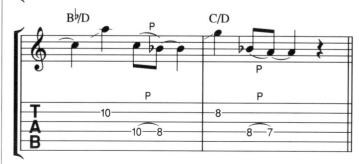

695

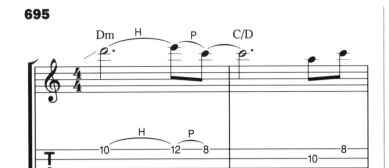

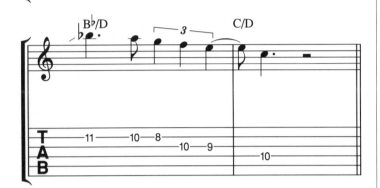

696

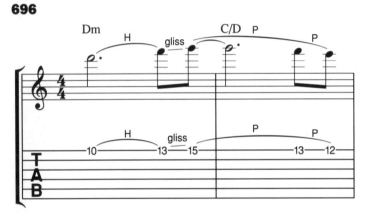

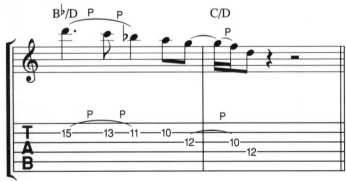

697

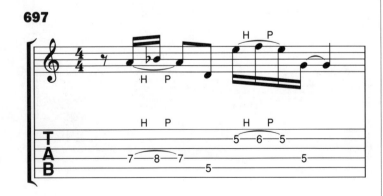

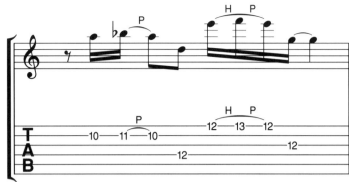

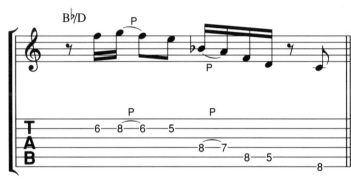

698

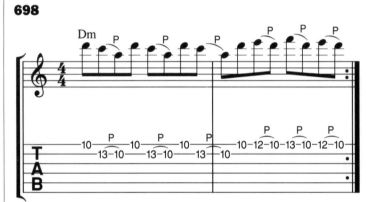

699

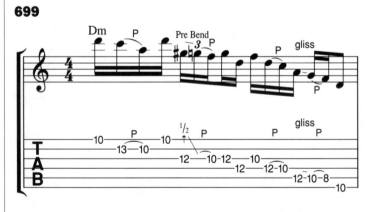

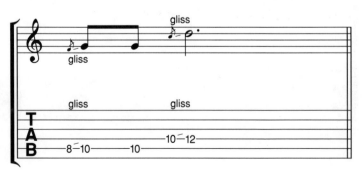

700

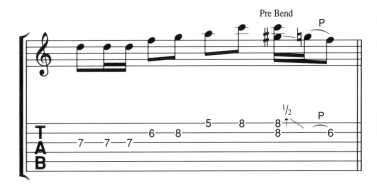

701

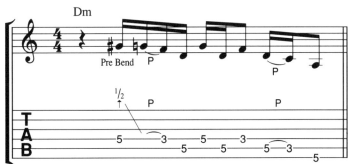

702

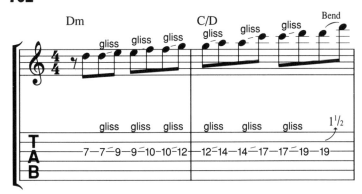

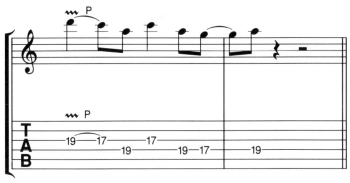

703

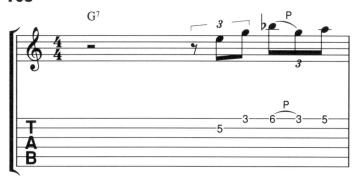

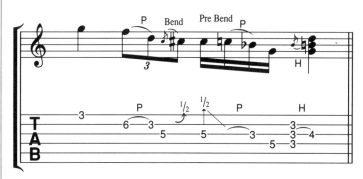

704

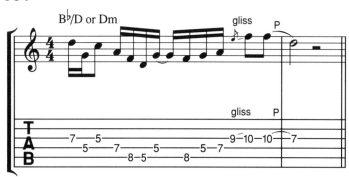

705

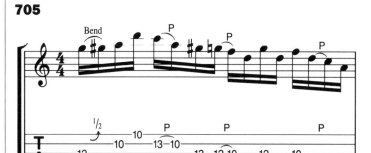

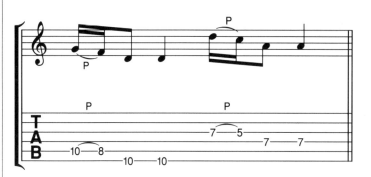

706

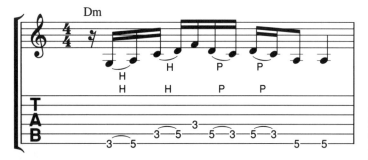

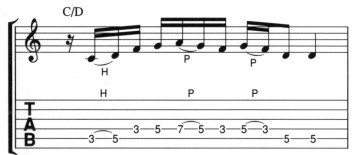

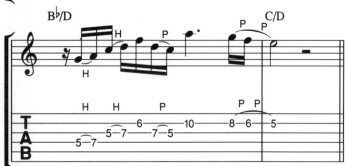

707

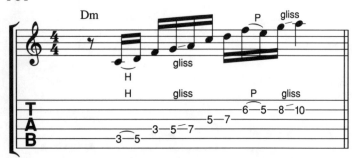

708

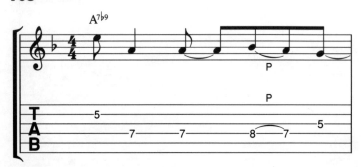

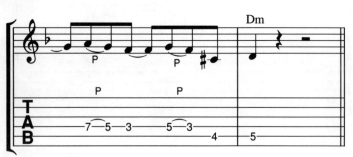

709

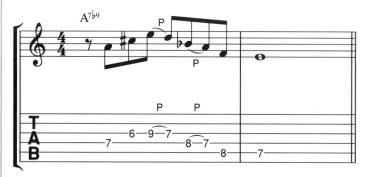

710

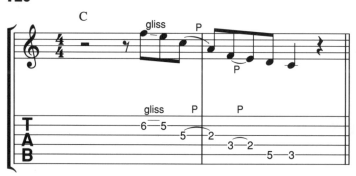

711

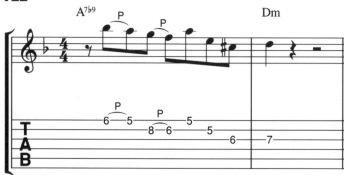

712

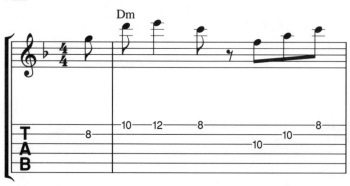

713

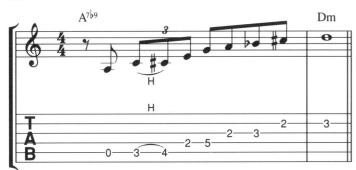

714

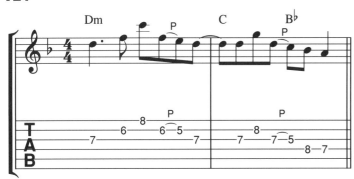

715

716

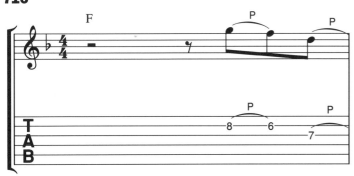

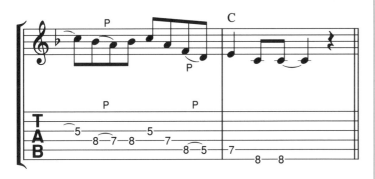

717

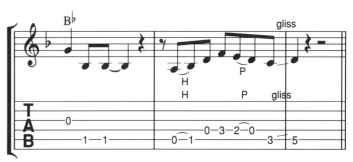

718

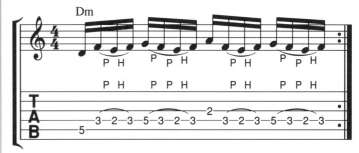

719

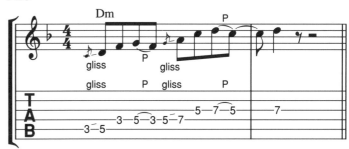

720

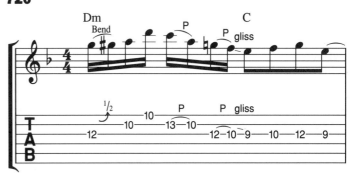

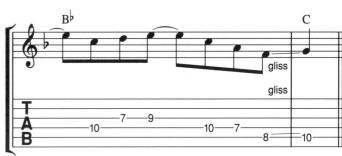

721

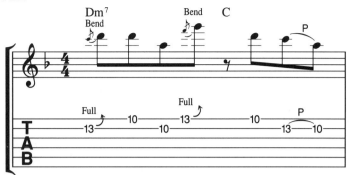

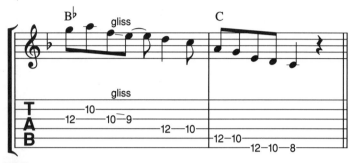

722

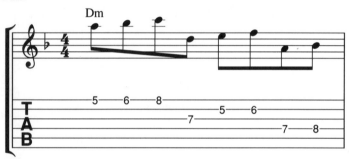

723

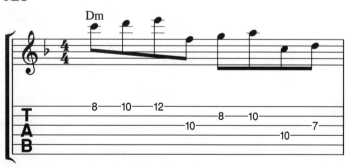

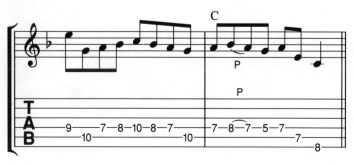

724

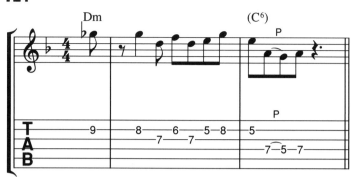

725

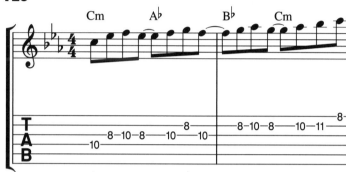

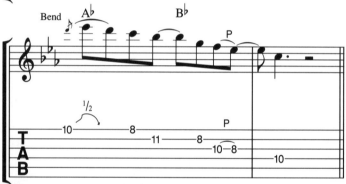

726

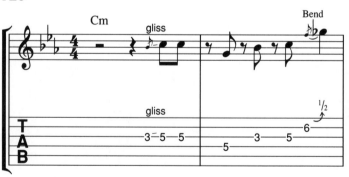

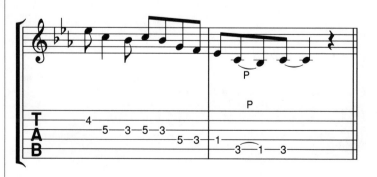

727

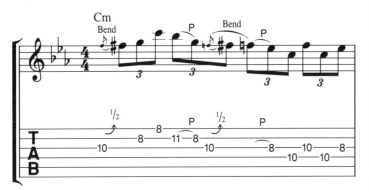

728

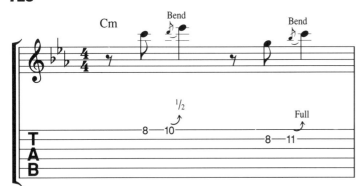

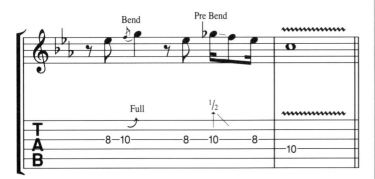

729

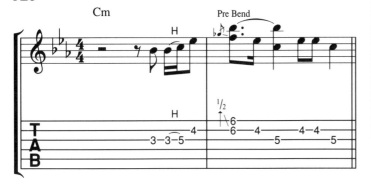

730

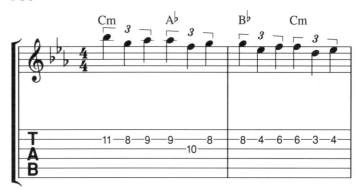

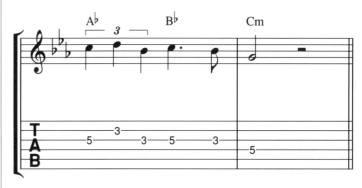

731

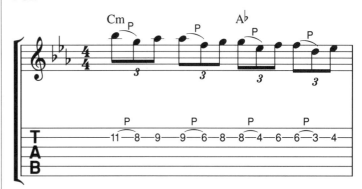

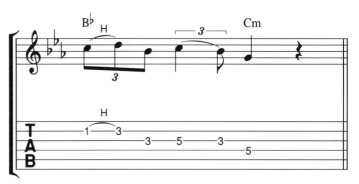

732

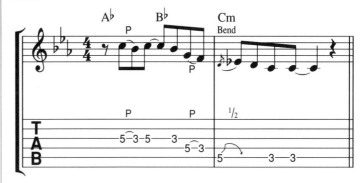

733

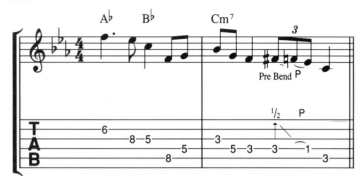

734

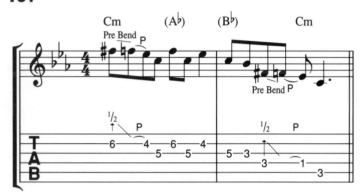

735

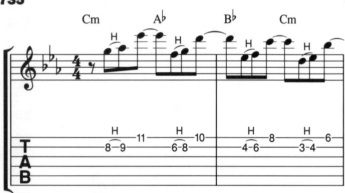

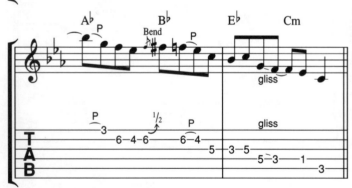

736

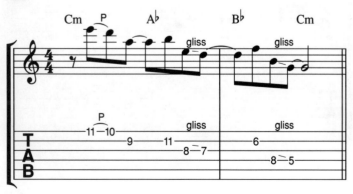

737

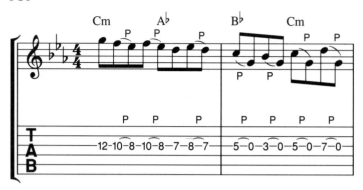

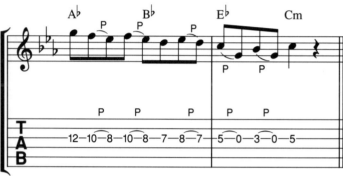

738

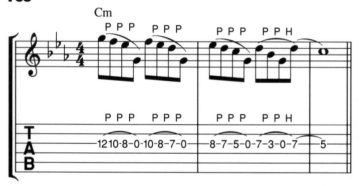

739

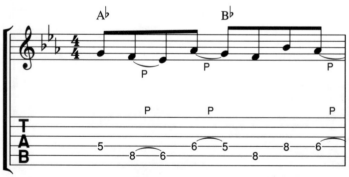

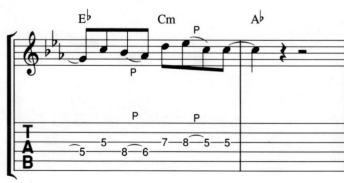

740

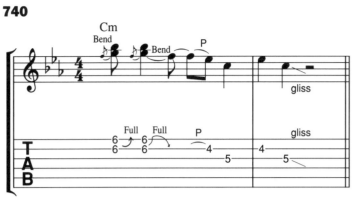

741

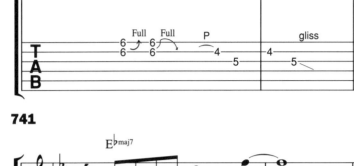

742

743

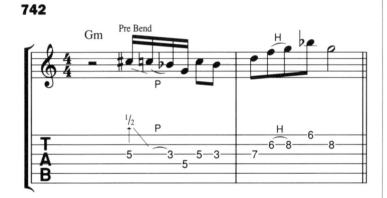

744

745

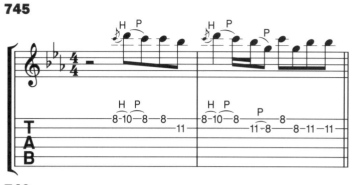

746

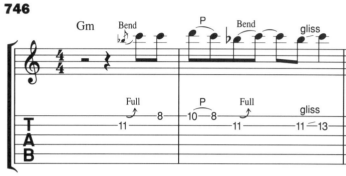

747

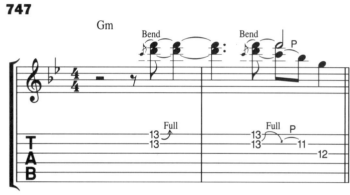

748

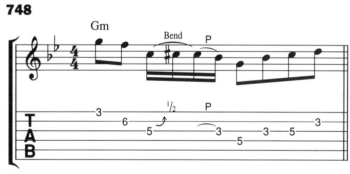

749

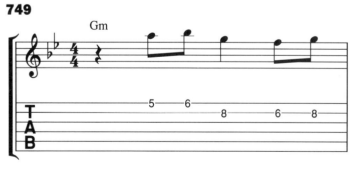

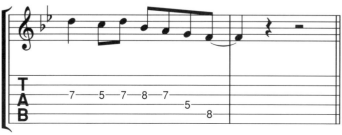

750

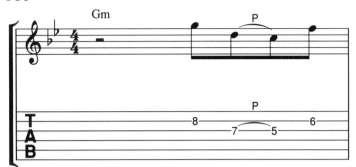

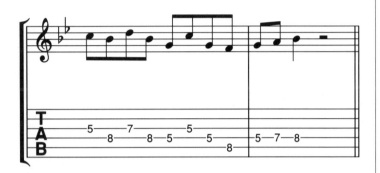

751

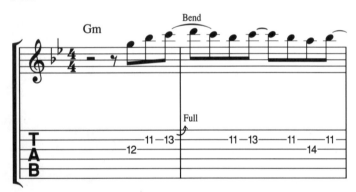

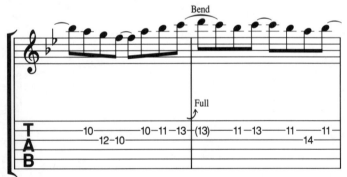

752

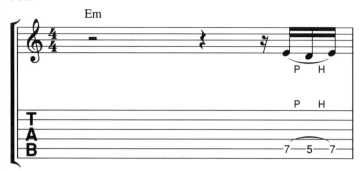

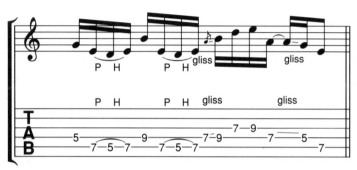

753

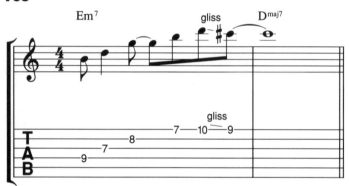

754

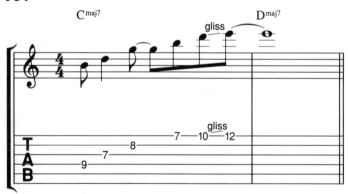

755

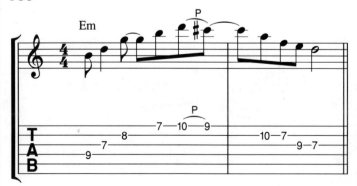

756

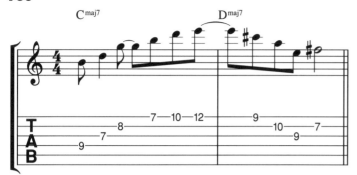

757

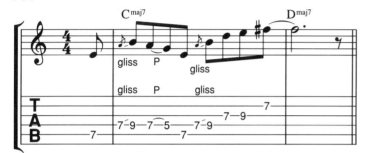

758

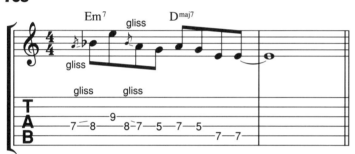

759

760

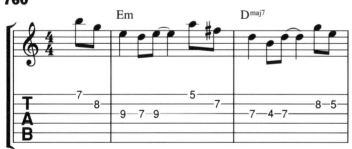

761

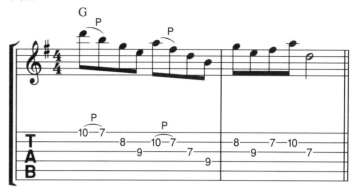

762

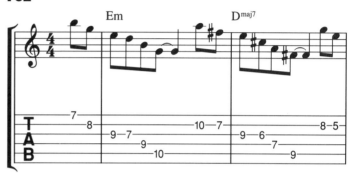

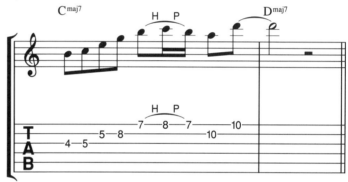

763

764

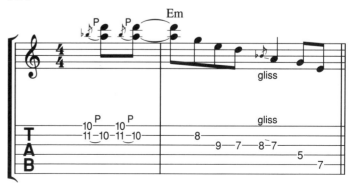

765

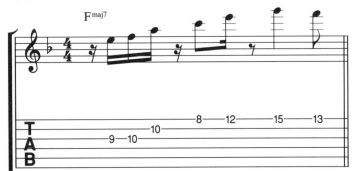

766

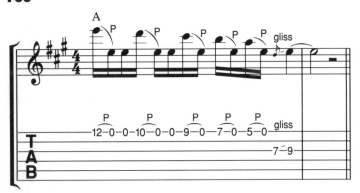

767

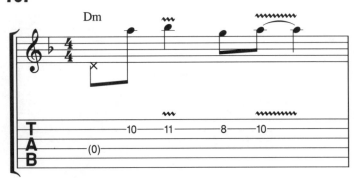

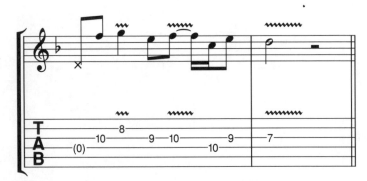

768

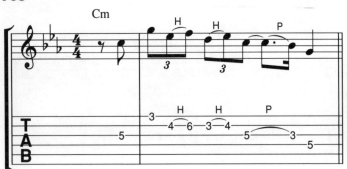

769

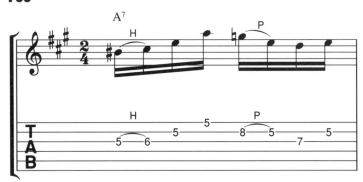

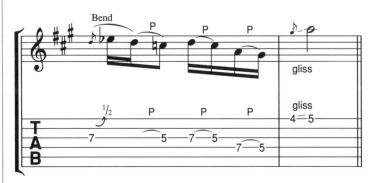

770

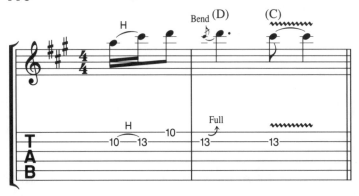

771

772

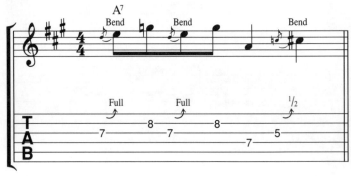

773

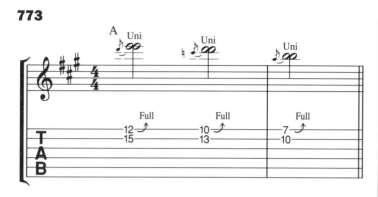

774

775

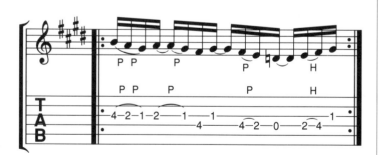

776

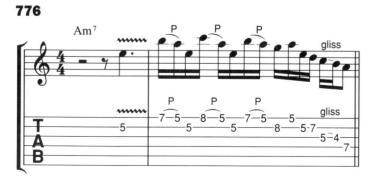

777

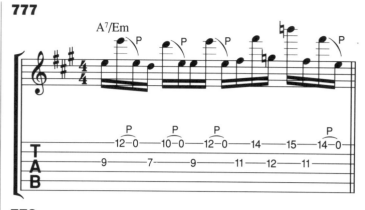

778

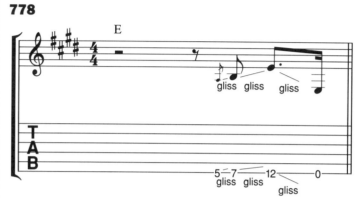

779

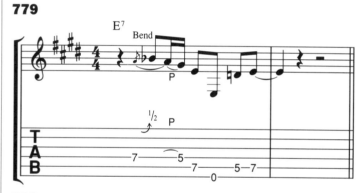

780

* Play this with the pick almost at a right angle to the strings for a rough, chugging sound.

781

* Play this one fingering the same left hand slur but press the whammy bar ¹/₂ step each time.

782

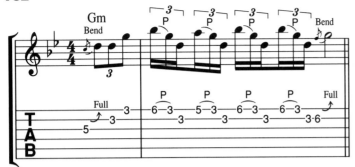

783

784

BLUES RIFFS

785

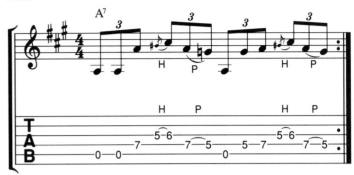

786

787

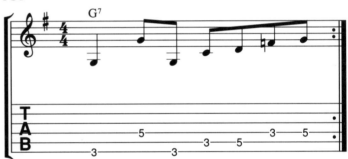

788 Now a slight variation.

789

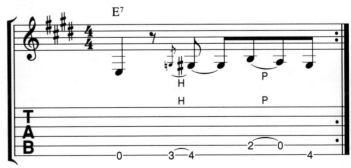

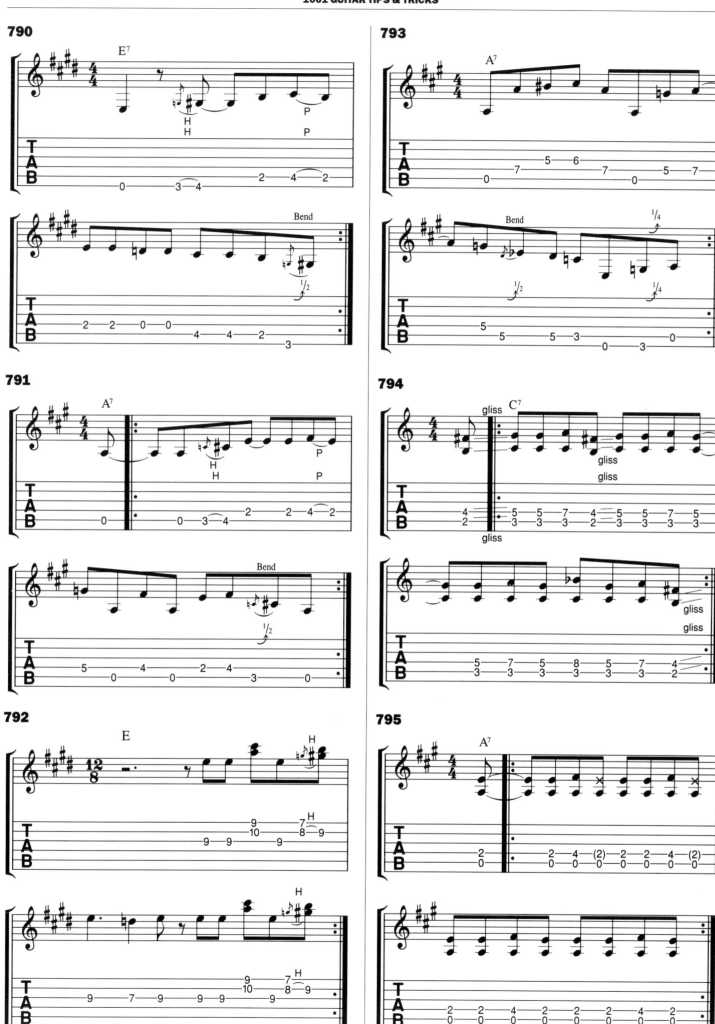

BLUES TURNAROUNDS

796 Last two bars of an E Blues.

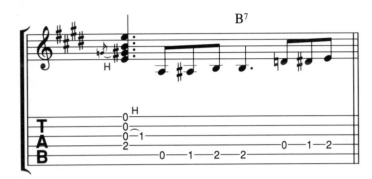

797 Last two bars of an E Blues.

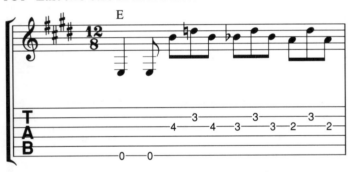

798

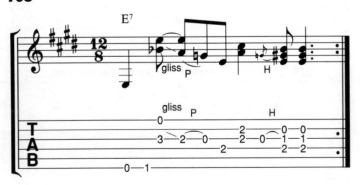

799

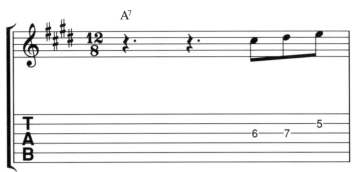

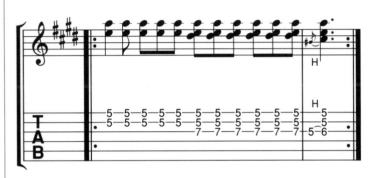

800

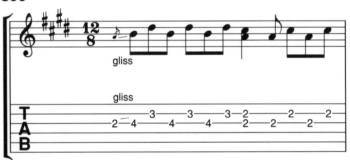

801

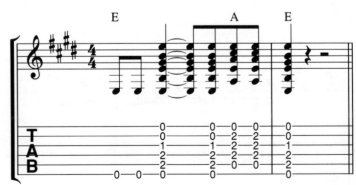

802

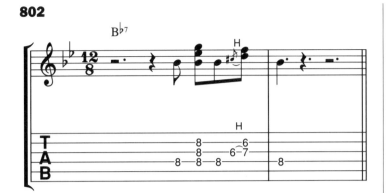

803

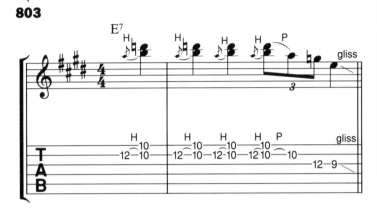

BLUES GUITAR LICKS

804

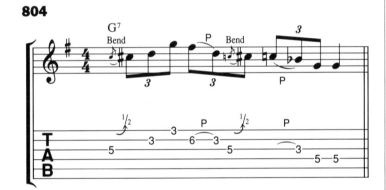

805

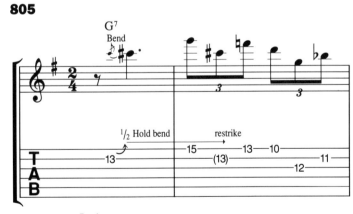

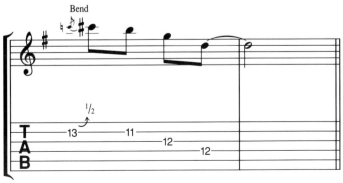

806

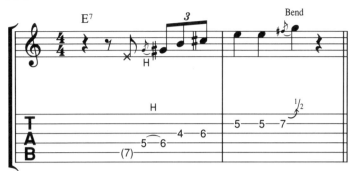

807

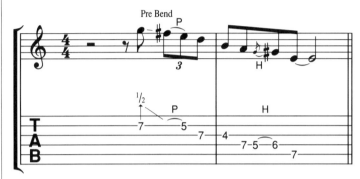

808

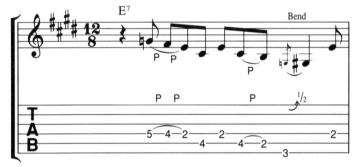

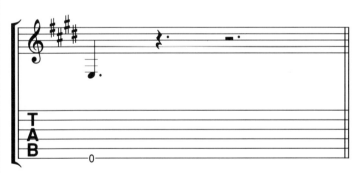

809

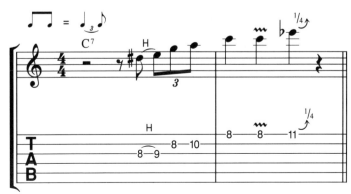

810

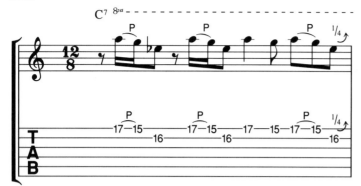

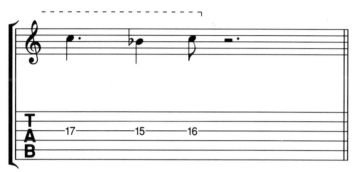

811

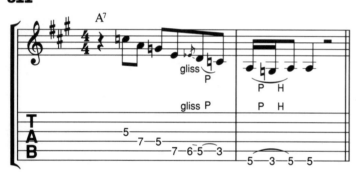

812

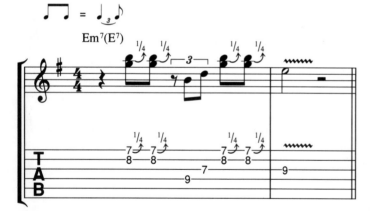

813

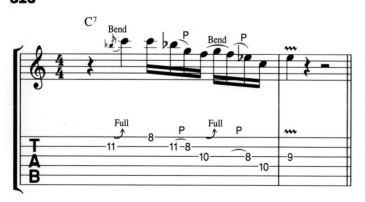

814

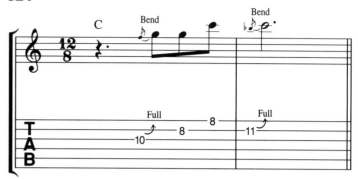

815

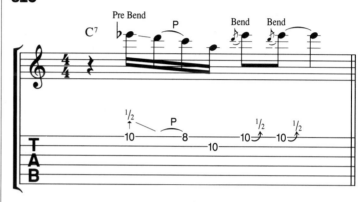

816 You can use a dead stop on the 11th bar of the last chorus (of a 12 bar blues) and put in a guitar fill.

817 For example:

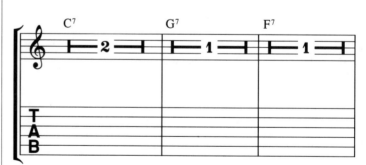

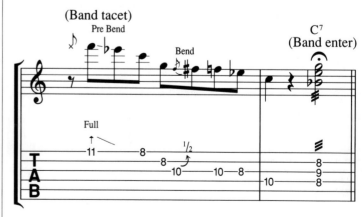

818

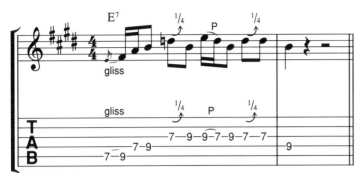

819

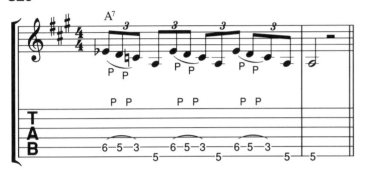

820 Try this over the 9th and 10th bars of a blues in C.

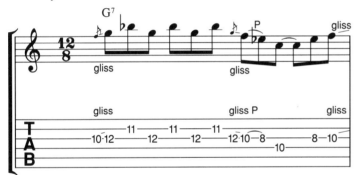

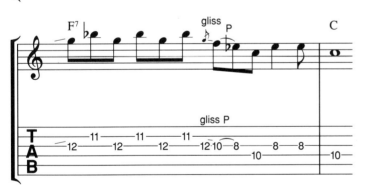

821

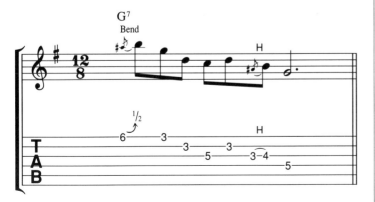

822

823

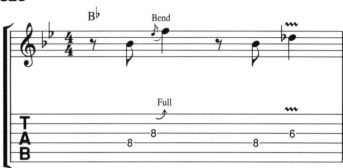

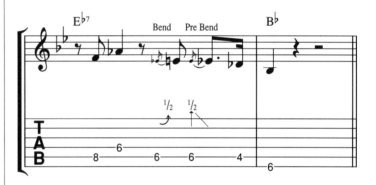

824

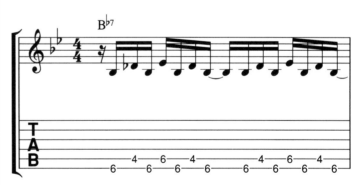

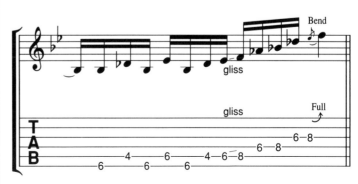

825

826

827

828

829

830

831

832

833

834

835

836

837

838

839

840 Now let's change a few notes to make this fit E♭7.

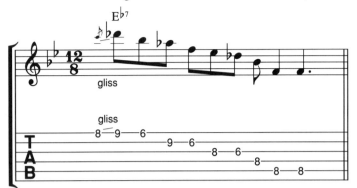

841

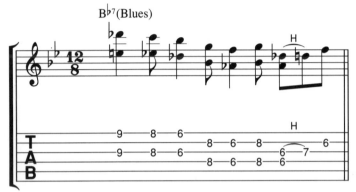

842 It's a little jazzy!

843 Maybe this one's in the wrong category too!

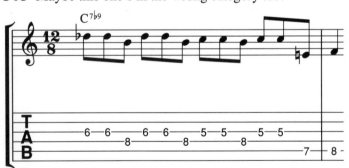

844

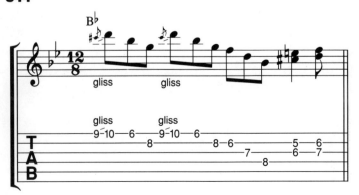

845 The next few examples come from a solo I wrote on a Gospel 12/8 version of 'Georgia'.

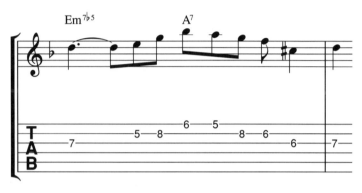

846

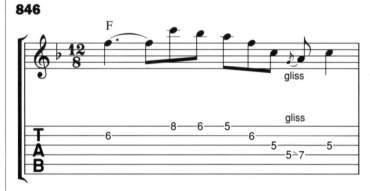

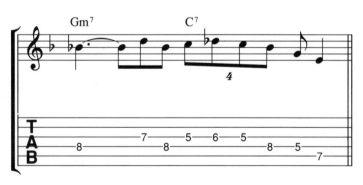

847

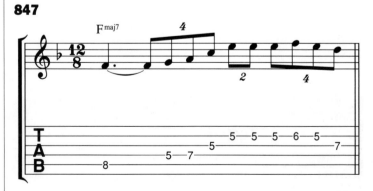

848

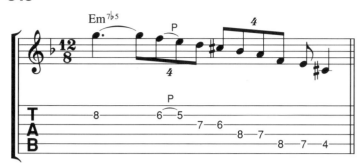

849

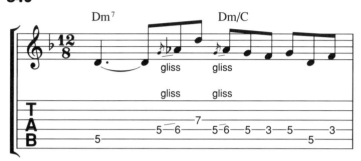

850

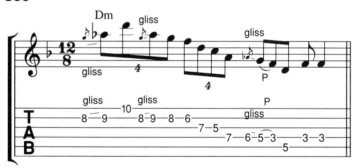

851

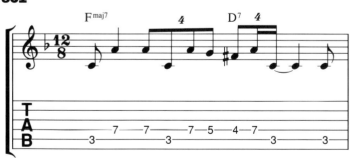

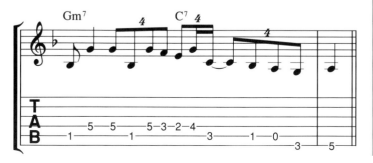

852

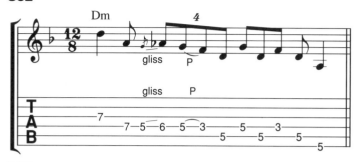

853

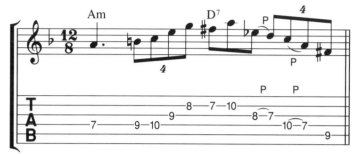

854

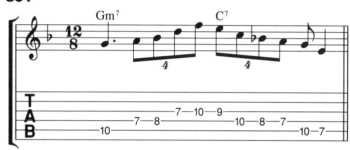

855 Notice the even sub-division of the beat.

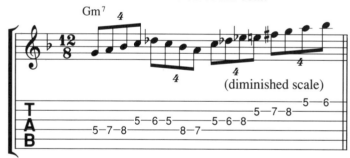

856

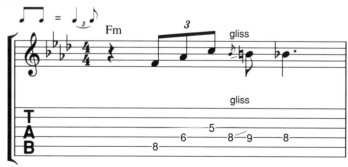

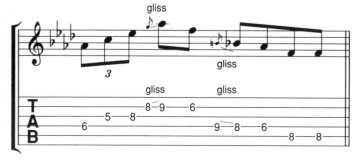

857

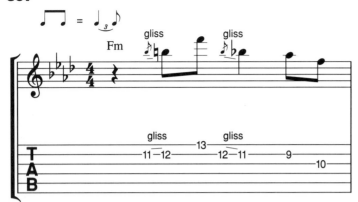

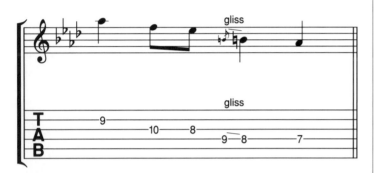

858

859

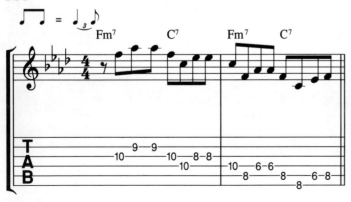

860

861

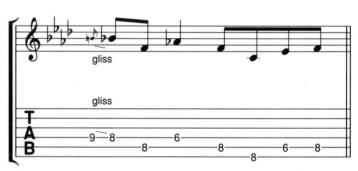

862 The rest of the solos in this section are in a Bebop or 'Jazz' Blues style.

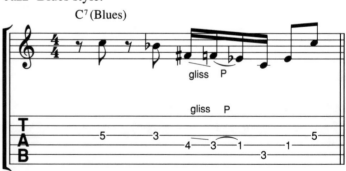

863

864

865

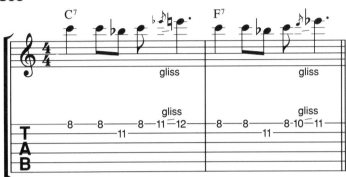

866

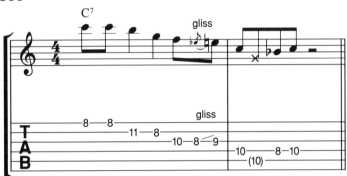

867

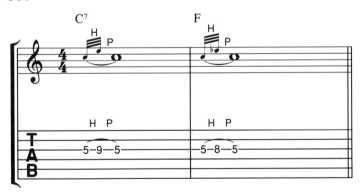

868

869

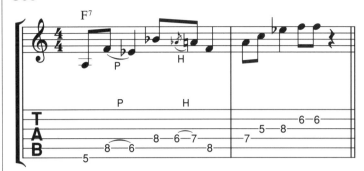

870

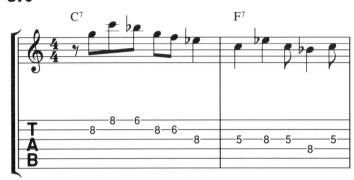

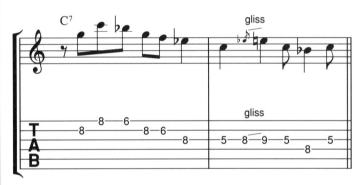

871

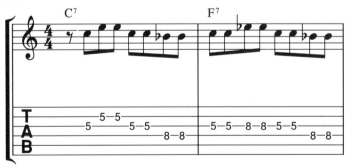

872

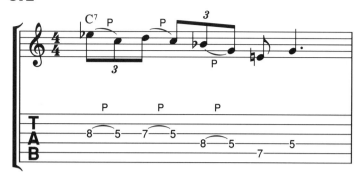

873

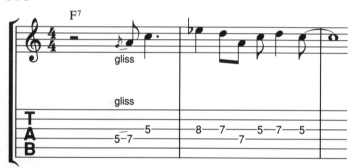

BLUES PROGRESSIONS

874 12-bar Blues in E

875 8-bar Blues in E

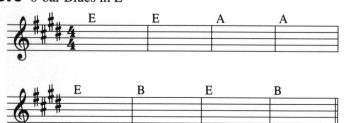

876 Most of these chords (if not all) should really be played as Dominant 7ths.

877 Jazz Blues in E

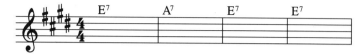

BLUES SCALES IN OPEN TUNINGS

878 Open E Blues scale tuning.

Tune guitar to E B E G# B E

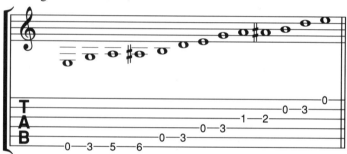

879 Open D Blues scale tuning.

Tune guitar to D A D F# A D

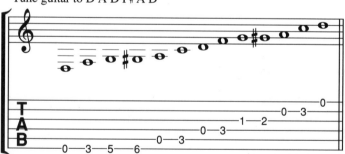

880 Open G tuning.

Tune guitar to D G D G B D

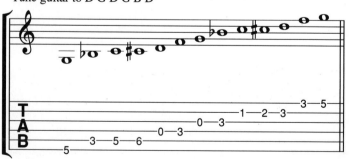

SLIDE GUITAR

SOME IDEAS IN STANDARD TUNING

881

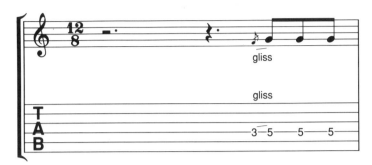

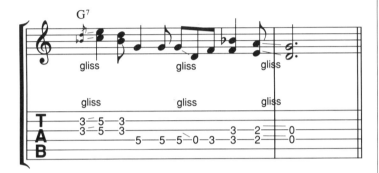

882 Try to execute the slide down to the open string cleanly.

883 You'll notice that vibrato is a very important part of good slide playing but don't overdo it.

Ry Cooder

COUNTRY GUITAR

884

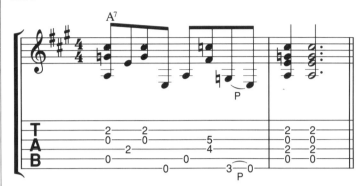

885

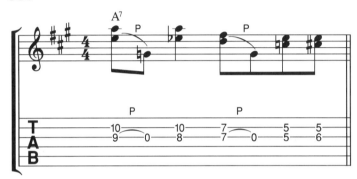

886

887

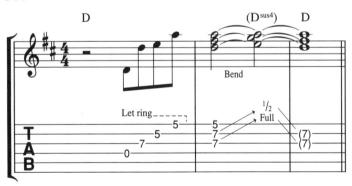

888

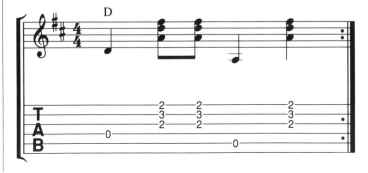

889

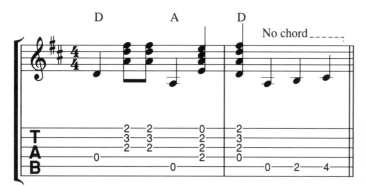

890

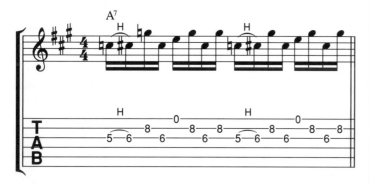

891

892

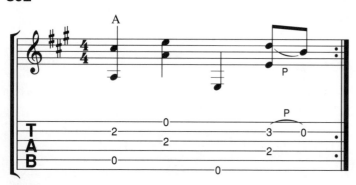

893

894

895

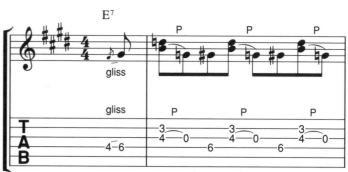

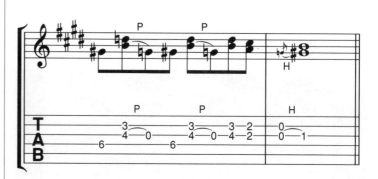

896

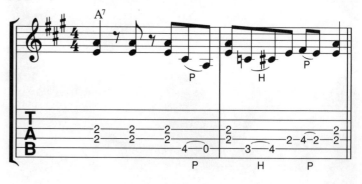

COUNTRY SOLOS

897

898

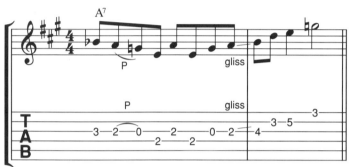

899

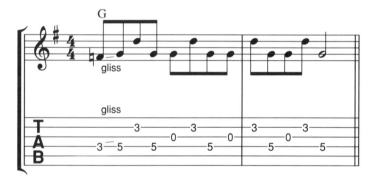

900

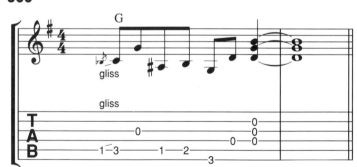

901

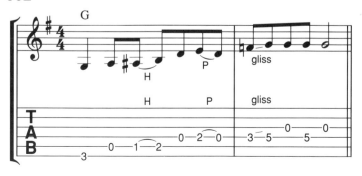

902

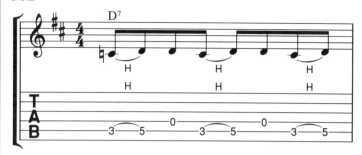

903

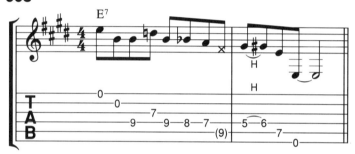

904

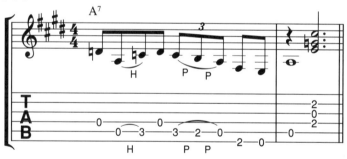

905

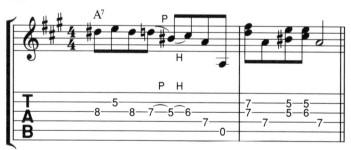

906

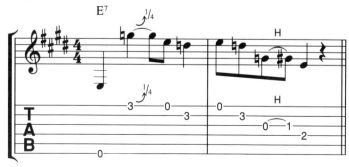

907

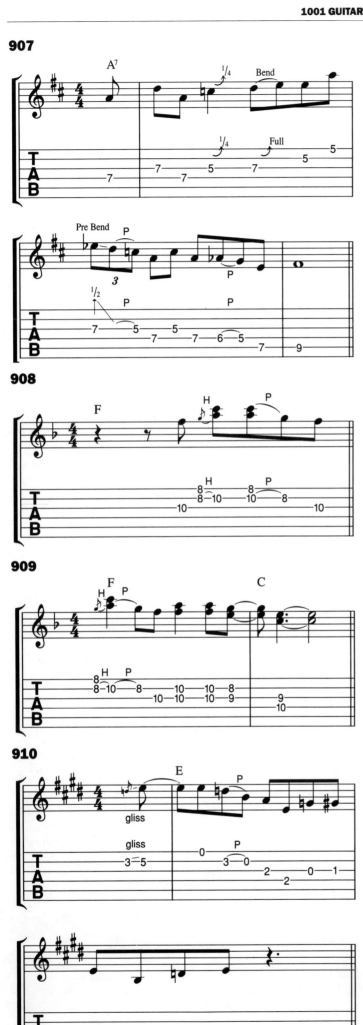

908

909

910

911

912

913

914

915

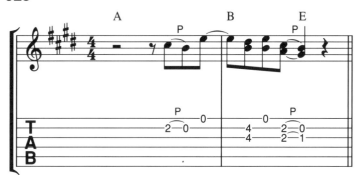

FUNKY RHYTHMS

919

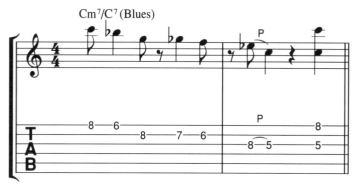

916

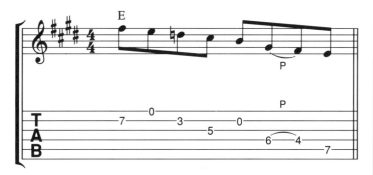

920

917

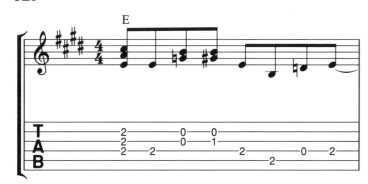

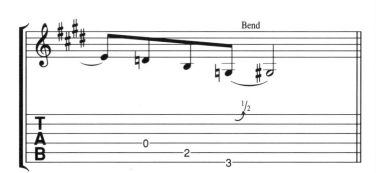

921

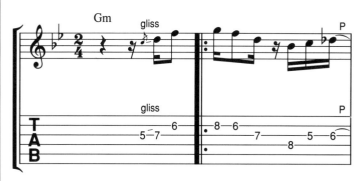

918

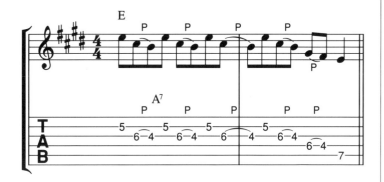

922

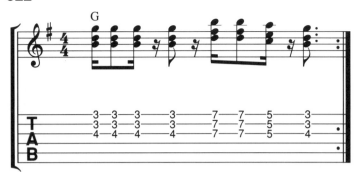

923 Soul Groove

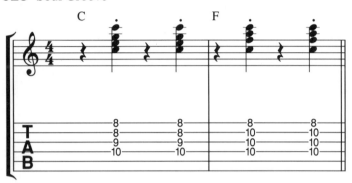

924 Reggae

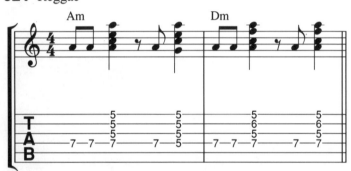

925

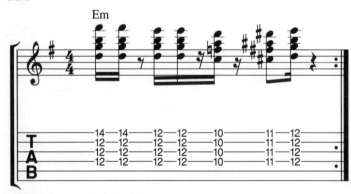

926

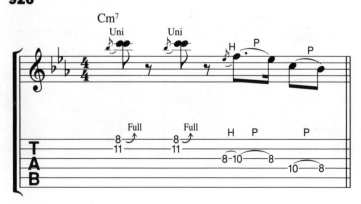

927

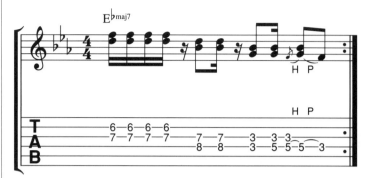

928

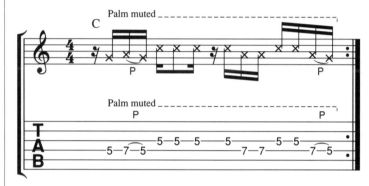

929

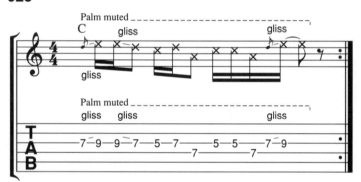

930

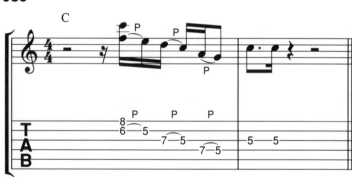

931

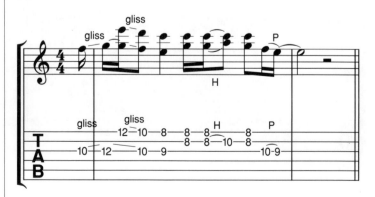

932

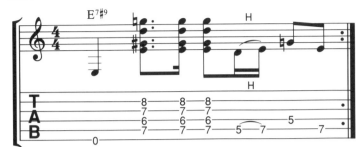

933

934

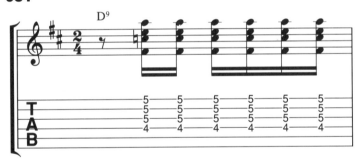

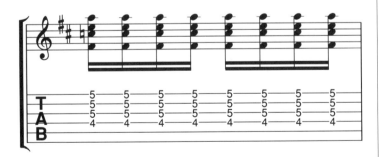

935

936

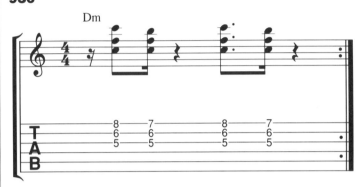

937 Note that, rather than muting the strings with your right hand, you can cut the notes short by lifting your left hand fingers quickly.

John Lee Hooker

JAZZ CHORDS

938

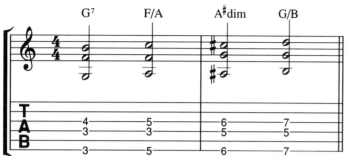

939

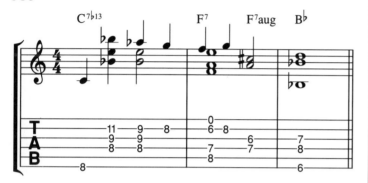

940 When presented with this melody:

you could try playing it in a chordal manner:

941 Add in some other moving notes.

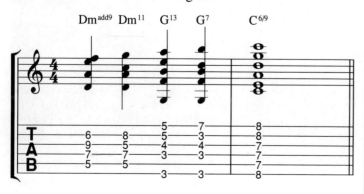

942 Now add an altered note E♭ (♭13 on G⁷).

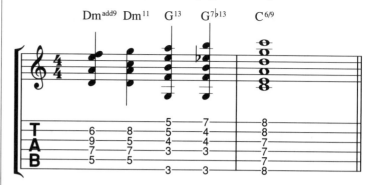

943 If you're playing in a setting where there's no other chordal instrument it's useful to be able to hit chords while playing a melody or solo.

944 Try this:

945 If you're accompanying a singer on a Latin tune (not a swing tune) you could try this kind of accompaniment.

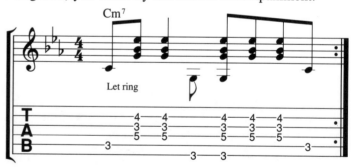

946 Here we use a first inversion of a chord (marked *) to make a smooth transition to the next chord. A first inversion is where the bottom note of the voicing is the third degree of the scale upon which the chord is based. E.g. G/B is a first inversion of the chord G with the third (B) in the bass.

JAZZ WALKING BASS

♪♪ = ♪₃♪ throughout this section.

947 Notes marked with * are chromatic passing notes, i.e. they are not found in the scale.

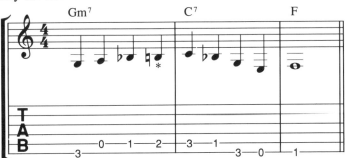

948

949

950 These bass lines always sound much more solid when the root of the chord is played on the first beat of the bar. To this end, you may often need to slip in chromatic passing notes. These are notes which are not found in the scales used but fill in the gap between two scale notes.

You'll probably notice that placing at least some of the chords on the off beat sounds a bit more jazzy.

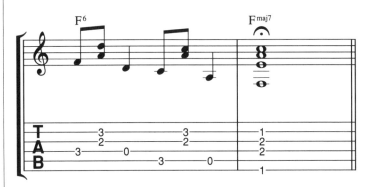

JAZZ SOLO IDEAS

♪♪ = ♪₃♪ throughout this section.

951 Playing a C major scale in octaves.

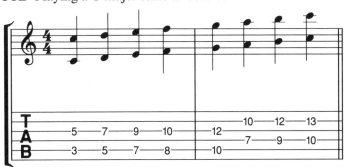

952 C Blues

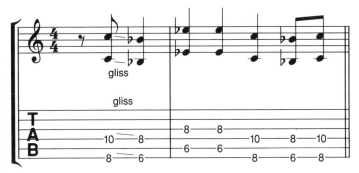

Pat Metheny

953 C/Cm Blues.

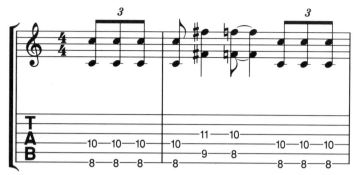

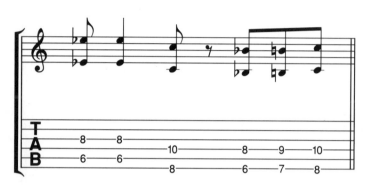

954

955

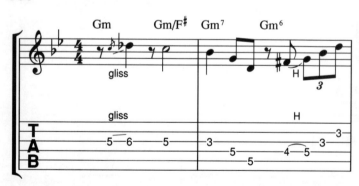

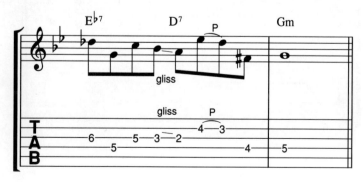

956

* Chromatic passing notes.

957

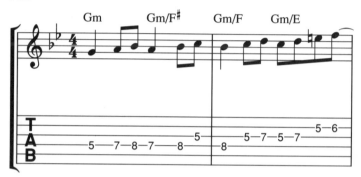

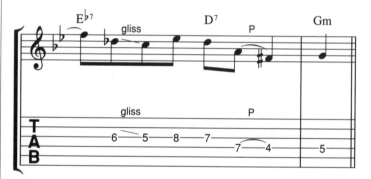

958

959 This one can be used as an ending.

960

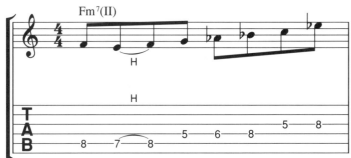

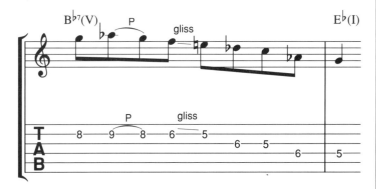

961

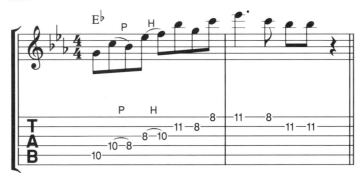

962

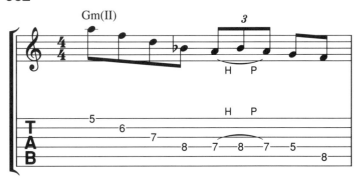

963

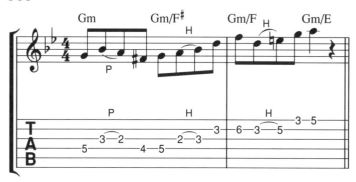

964

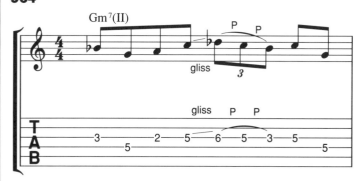

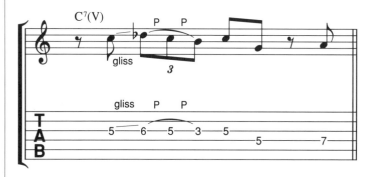

965

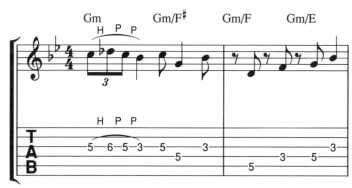

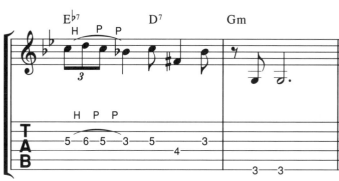

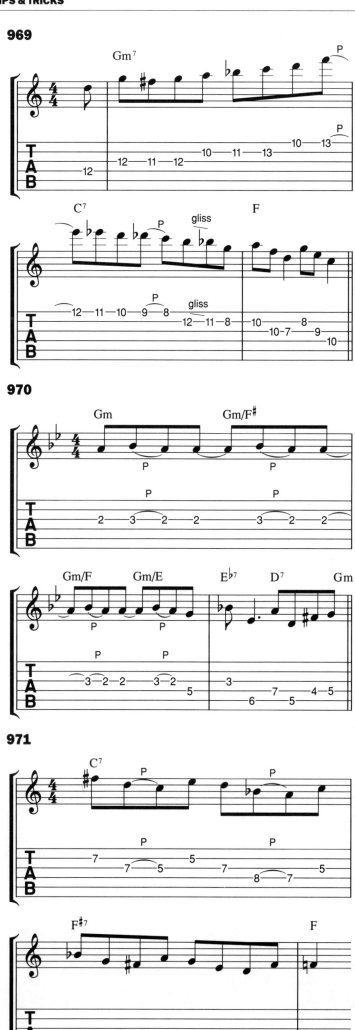

972

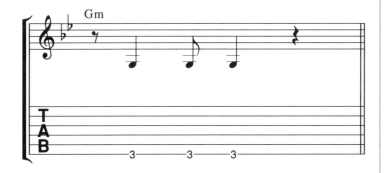

973

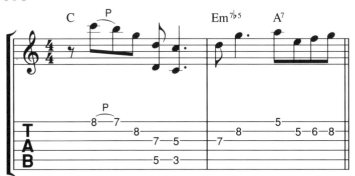

974

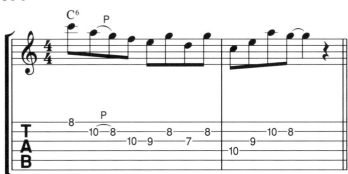

975

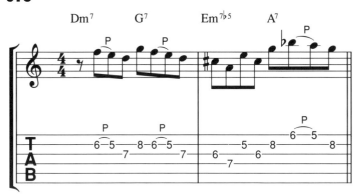

976

977

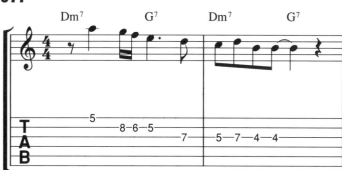

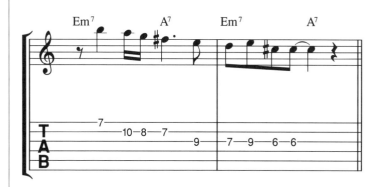

978

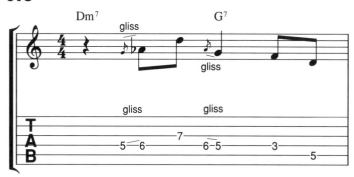

979

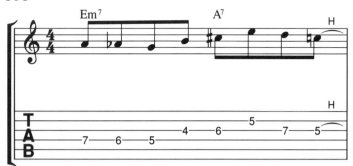

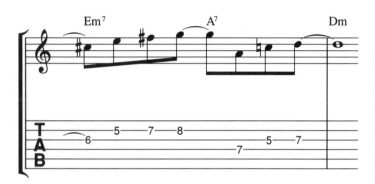

980

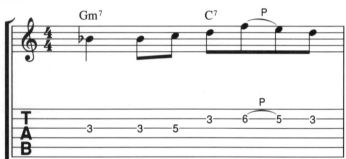

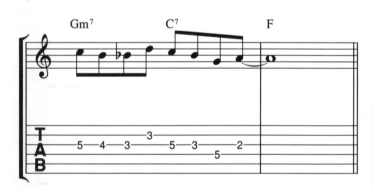

981

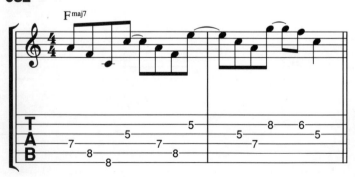

982

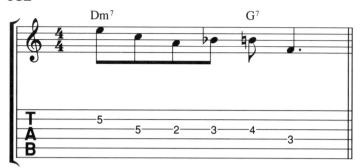

983

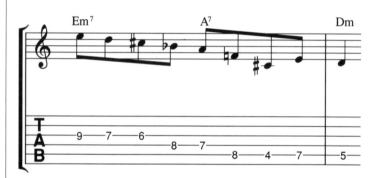

984 This is a stock ending for a jazz tune.

985 This is a stock ending for a jazz tune.

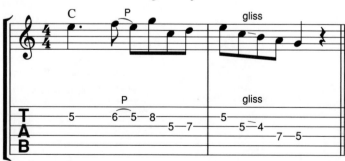

986

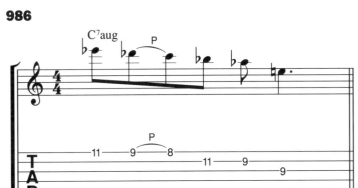

987

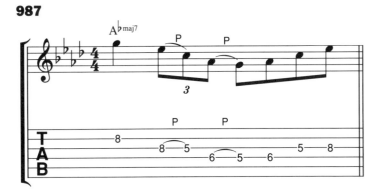

988

989

990

991

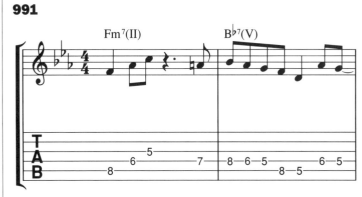

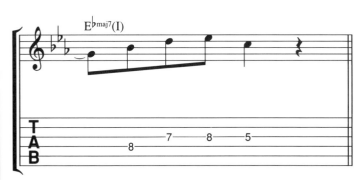

992

993

994

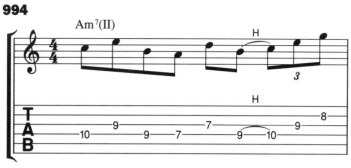

995

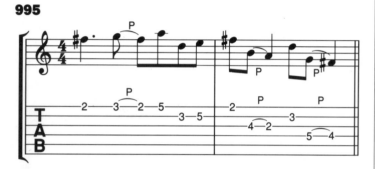

996

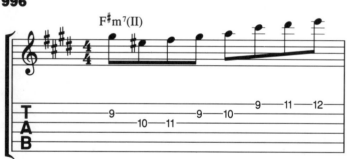

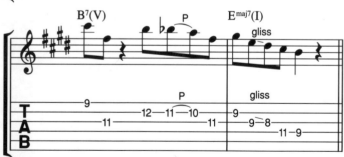

997

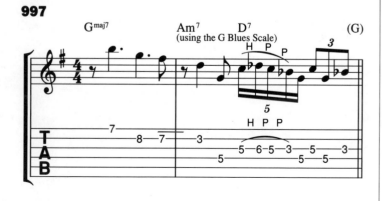

998

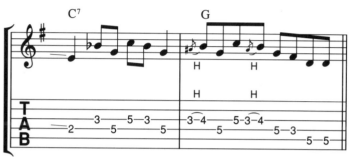

999

1000

1001

The Beatles

Enya

Phil Collins

Van Morrison

Bob Dylan

Sting

Paul Simon

Tracy Chapman

Eric Clapton

Pink Floyd

New Kids On The Block

Bryan Adams

Tina Turner

Elton John

Bee Gees

Whitney Houston

AC/DC

Bringing you the words

All the latest in rock and pop. Plus the brightest and best in West End show scores. Music books for every instrument under the sun. And exciting new teach-yourself ideas like "Let's Play Keyboard" - in cassette/book packs, or on video. Available from all good music shops.

and music

Music Sales' complete catalogue lists thousands of titles and is available free from your local music shop, or direct from Music Sales Limited. Please send a cheque or postal order for £1.50 (for postage) to:

Music Sales Limited
Newmarket Road,
Bury St Edmunds,
Suffolk IP33 3YB

Buddy

Five Guys Named Moe

Les Misérables

West Side Story

Phantom Of The Opera

Show Boat

The Rocky Horror Show

Bringing you the world's best music.